The Noah Generation:
The Sign of Revival Rain

Kevin M. Rice

The Noah Generation:

The Sign of Revival Rain

Copyright © 2022 by Kevin M. Rice. All Rights Reserved.

All rights reserved. No part of this book may be reproduced in any form or by any electronic or mechanical means, including information storage and retrieval systems, without permission in writing from the Author. The only exception is a reviewer, who may quote short excerpts in a review.

Cover design Iram S. Author's Photo by Racheal Mahon

Kevin M. Rice

Visit our website at www.EternalKingdomInternational.com

Printed in the United States of America

Crown City, OH

First Printing: July 2023

Eternal Kingdom International Publishing, LLC

LIBRARY OF CONGRESS

LCCN: 2022940897

ISBN- 978-1-7341088-3-5 - Paperback

ISBN- 978-1-7341088-4-2 - eBook

ISBN- 978-1-7341088-6-6 - Hardback

ISBN- 978-1-7341088-5-9 – Audio

Copyright © 2023

All rights reserved.

Printed in the United States of Americ

But of that day and hour knoweth no man, no, not the angels of heaven, but my Father only. But as the days of Noe were, so shall also the coming of the Son of man be. For as in the days that were before the flood they were eating and drinking, marrying and giving in marriage, until the day that Noe entered into the Ark, And knew not until the flood came, and took them all away; so shall also the coming of the Son of man be.

- Matthew 24: 36-39 (KJV) JESUS CHRIST

Dedication:

Over the years, my wife and our family have gone through many struggles. We have seen highs and lows in ministry and life. Some topics in this book were based on conversations with a minister friend, Miguel Escobar, who passed away before this book was written.

I would love to dedicate this book to everyone who has touched my life, both in the ministry and in the necessity of life itself. Pages could not convey my gratitude for the friendships and encouragement I have received from so many.

In this life, we may not always receive the words of thanks and praise we desire, but if we look back over our lives and see those who have walked the road with us, we see the true gifts we have been given.

Life is not about the awards and accolades of man but about the impact you make in the eternity of others. We press towards a prize, not of this world but one that is eternal. Seek the King and His Kingdom, and you will discover the blessings this life has already given you.

Thank you to all the readers. Enjoy that great adventure that awaits you ahead.

Kevin M. Rice

Foreword

Through vibrant allegories and practical truths, Kevin M. Rice elevates our perspective on where we are as a generation and how we must respond to our current spiritual environment. The Noah Generation is a timely message and a must-read for those who desire to hear more clearly what the Lord is presently speaking to the church.

The revival the church has been looking for and waiting on for centuries is upon us. The role the church is to play in this latter-day outpouring has been outlined with great care throughout the pages of this text. It is time for the church to understand the role we have to play. We have been placed in the Kingdom of Heaven for such a time as this, and the manifestation of this end-time revival rest upon our shoulders.

Many have looked into the nature of the generation of Noah's day, but few have given such a clear understanding and insight into how our present generation fits into the analogy Christ used in Matthew 24.

This book provides great insight and applications into how we can change our mindset and worldview and step into the role God has ordained for His Church. Come join the authors as they take you on a journey into the great adventure God has ordained for His Church, and join Kevin on this amazing journey into the Noah generation.

By Chuck Lawrence
Senior Pastor Christ Temple Church
Huntington WV.

Contents

Introduction 1

Chapter One 3

Chapter Two 16

Chapter Three 32

Chapter Four 45

Chapter Five 58

Chapter Six 81

Chapter Seven 98

Chapter Eight 115

Chapter Nine 129

The Coming of the Lord

Introduction

Watch therefore: for ye know not what hour your Lord doth come.
Matthew 24: 42 (KJV)

The coming of the Lord is an event the church has been anticipating for two centuries. Jesus taught about the coming of the Lord on many occasions. In one particular instance, He gave reference to the generation of Noah. Considering the time of Noah before the writing of the Bible, little details exist as to what that generation was like. In a similar teaching, Jesus compared these times to those of Lot, Jonah, and Noah. If we look at these three stories in the Old Testament, we discover that the outcome of Jonah's time was far different from those of Noah and Lot.

Join us on a journey through the scriptures as we discover what it was like during the generation of Noah and the correlations to the prophecies spoken by Christ. The coming revival is contingent on our ability to recognize the similarities between our time and the generation of Noah.

The desire to leave this world for a better home is in the heart of every believer, but we cannot leave until the task given to us is complete. Many scriptures point to the tasks left in our hands to complete before the coming of the Lord. These tasks are contingent upon our understanding of the signs of the time and the generation of Noah.

What the world needs is not a mass exodus of the religious people but a manifestation of the Holy Ghost-filled church of God. It is time for the church to manifest the Kingdom of heaven with signs and wonders. The world needs the sons of God operating in the power and demonstration of the Holy Ghost.

It is not time to sit back, hiding from the world until the Lord returns. There are specific tasks that we must complete before the Lord returns. Join us as we discover the path to revival rain and the signs associated with the Noah Generation.

The Days of Noah

Chapter One

By faith Noah, being warned of God of things not seen as yet, moved with fear, prepared an ark to the saving of his house; by the which he condemned the world, and became heir of the righteousness which is by faith.

Hebrews 11:7 (KJV)

Jesus was sitting upon the Mount of Olives when he began to teach His disciples about things to come. Christ tells them about the signs of the time and the coming of the Son of Man.

During this conversation, Jesus makes the following analogy

> *But of that day and hour knoweth no man, no, not the angels of heaven, but my Father only. But as the days of Noe were, so shall also the coming of the Son of man be. For as in the days that were before the flood they were eating and drinking, marrying and giving in marriage, until the day that Noe entered into the Ark, And knew not until the flood came, and took them all away; so shall also the coming of the Son of man be.*
>
> *Matthew 24: 36 -39(KJV)*

Many people have attempted to draw correlations between the times of Noah and the wickedness of today. There is a significant body of evidence to support similarities. In truth, referencing today's culture and the Biblical culture described in Genesis is identical. Today every kind of depravity is routine. Homosexuality, hatred, wrath, murder, wickedness, immorality, and such are so commonplace that even our children have become desensitized to corruption.

> *And GOD saw that the wickedness of man was great in the earth, and that every imagination of the thoughts of his heart was only evil continually.*
>
> Genesis 6:5 (KJV)

If we look closely at the passage of scripture from the Gospel of Matthew above and that found in Luke, we find there are four things Christ used to define these times.

> *And as it was in the days of Noe, so shall it be also in the days of the Son of man. They did eat, they drank, they married wives, they were given in marriage, until the day that Noe entered into the Ark, and the flood came, and destroyed them all. Likewise also as it was in the days of Lot; they did eat, they drank, they bought, they sold, they planted, they builded;*

> *But the same day that Lot went out of Sodom it rained fire and brimstone from heaven, and destroyed them all. Even thus shall it be in the day when the Son of man is revealed.*
>
> Luke 17: 26-30 (KJV)

Jesus indicated that the characteristics of the times of Noah were eating, drinking, marrying, and giving in marriage. Jesus doesn't imply the sign of the coming of the Son of Man is the wickedness of the generation. This leaves us with a puzzle. What was the sign Jesus was signifying that would be indicative of this generation?

Let's consider the four criteria that Jesus used to define the times of Noah and the time of Lot. We discover that these four criteria are always present with us. Men have been eating, drinking, marrying, and giving their daughters in marriage from the beginning of time.

We can say the same about the wickedness of man. From the times of Noah until today, wickedness has been with us. In fact, homosexuality appears to have been present right after the Ark of Noah had landed, and Ham, Noah's son, did something to Noah while he was naked and asleep. This action must have been so inappropriate that Noah cursed the descendants of Ham. (Gen. 9:20-27).

Homosexuality also appeared in Lots time, but it was not unique to those times; it was prevalent in the whole land of Canaan and the tribe of Benjamin (Judges 19).

The history of man has had times of great darkness and times of purity. However, wickedness has always co-existed with mankind from the fall. Each generation says that their generation is worse than any before. Nevertheless, is watching for evil to increase what Christ is teaching at this point to His disciples?

For a moment, let us look at the generation of Noah from a strictly logistical standpoint. A man having three sons is in the middle of a building project that he says was given to him by God. The project is to build a boat to house all the animals and protect them from an imminent flood.

Let us pause for just a second. A flood? According to some theologians (Genesis 2:5–6), it had never rained before the flood. However, Dr. Tommy Mitchell at Answersingenesis.org indicates insufficient scriptural evidence to support this line of thought. However, in "The Book of Enoch," translated by R.H. Charles, [1917] (Chapter 76:6, 8-12), albeit not canonical, rain is mentioned at a time before the flood. If we take into account the observation of rain in "The Book of Enoch," we cannot conclude that the appearance of rain clouds in the sky was the omen that marked the sign of the time of Noah.

Let us go back to our observations from the times of Noah. A man with a message from God, building a massive structure for an impending flood with his family. This construction could have taken about 55 to 75 years (Anwersingenesis.org). While constructing the Ark, he preached righteousness (2 Peter 2:5). Then came the collecting of the animals into the Ark. I am sure this event did not go unnoticed by the generation of Noah. Was this the sign?

We can conclude that Noah's generation saw three undeniable events/signs before the flood. The first was a message of salvation. The second was the construction of the means of their salvation. And the third was the gathering of a massive congregation to be saved.

As the generation of Noah lived out their lives, these events were taking place. They were not concerned with the activities of Noah. They were not even moved by the message that was preached. They went about their daily business and lived their everyday lives. All the while, the signs were all around them.

As Noah built the Ark, his concern was not that of his generation. His concern was the salvation of his children. He did not look for a sign of the flood to come. All he had was a word that destruction was imminent. He had the designs for the Ark, and his focus was to build the plan for salvation before time was out.

Today, however, the religious church world is looking for a sign. They are looking to the sky for signs in the heavens. They are watching the wickedness of the world around them for a sign. Is it not funny that the more you look for wickedness, the more you see it? The same can be said about signs in the heavens.

Sometimes I wonder if the church world is not looking at the world's wickedness out of envy and jealousy. They can list the world's sins more readily than the miracles that God has done in the last week. It makes you wonder if, in their heart, they are only living religiously to get out of this world and not go to hell. Nevertheless, their heart is envious of those who can fulfill the lust of their flesh without fear.

Jesus taught that those looking for a sign would never receive one.

> *A wicked and adulterous generation seeketh after a sign; and there shall no sign be given unto it, but the sign of the prophet Jonas. And he left them, and departed.*
>
> *Matthew 16:14 (KJV)*

What was the sign of Jonah? Are there any similarities between Jonah and Noah?

When we examine Jonah and Nineveh, we see the same three events/signs found in the time of Noah. A preacher showed up. He may not have smelled that great, but the sign was a preacher calling for repentance. The plan was given; "repent." Then the city gathered to be saved.

In the passage of Luke we presented earlier, Jesus mentioned the time of Lot. Do these same three events/signs appear in the story of Lot?

When we examine Lot's story, we find that a message is sent to Lot. Three angels arrive at Sodom with a message of impending destruction. Lot is given a plan to escape. Those to be saved are gathered and left the city before the destruction begins.

In light of all these correlations to the events outlined in Noah's generation, Lot's generation, and Jonah's generation today, what is the church doing today? The church claims to be gathering "those who are to be saved." However, they are looking for a sign to guide them. They spend countless hours trying to discern the signs of the time and neglect the salvation of the generation to which they have been called.

What has turned people's eyes away from the work at hand? What have they looked for as a sign of the coming of the Son of Man? The field is ripe, and the laborers are few. When you talk to the members of churches today, you hear all kinds of excuses. The underlying root of these excuses is a lack of understanding of the purpose of the church. The unwillingness to take on the responsibility given to the church by the commission of Jesus Christ leaves the church wandering without purpose.

It reminds you of a slothful farmer who looked outside and said to himself, "It looks like it'll rain today. I will work my field tomorrow." Harvest time came, but the crops did not.

> *He that observeth the wind shall not sow; and he that regardeth the clouds shall not reap.*
>
> *Ecclesiastes 11:4 (KJV)*

The Bible talks about the slothful and their nature.

The slothful man saith, There is a lion in the way; a lion is in the streets. As the door turneth upon his hinges, so doth the slothful upon his bed. The slothful hideth his hand in his bosom; it grieveth him to bring it again to his mouth.

Proverbs 26: 13-15 (KJV)

Is there a spirit of slothfulness in the church today? Are they looking for a sign that the Lord is coming to get out of the task of reaching the lost?

Let us look at a message Jesus taught the disciples while referring to the days of Noah in Matthew chapter 24.

Then shall two be in the field; the one shall be taken, and the other left. Two women shall be grinding at the mill; the one shall be taken, and the other left.

Matthew 24: 40- 41 (KJV)

Jesus is not teaching the disciples to pull out of the world and hide in remote places. He is not telling them they will be lost if they have a secular job and work with an unbeliever. The type of jobs Jesus refers to in this passage are common to man. He is not telling them to all go out and be a preacher, or if they are not in the ministry, they will not be taken.

Based on this statement being at work in and with the world appears to be a requirement. Those people who fear the world and hide from interacting with it for fear they may be negatively impacted have no excuse.

Let's take the three criteria we listed above and apply them to our day. We should be interacting with the world to tell them about the way of salvation. We can preach in a church building all day long, and the message never reaches those who need to hear it until we take it to them.

Let us look a little further:

> *Watch therefore: for ye know not what hour your Lord doth come. But know this, that if the goodman of the house had known in what watch the thief would come, he would have watched, and would not have suffered his house to be broken up. Therefore be ye also ready: for in such an hour as ye think not the Son of man cometh.*
>
> *Matthew 24:42-44 (KJV)*

I hear the reader's mind saying, "Ok, we need to be looking for the coming of the Lord; there is the proof." However, is that truly what is being said?

In verse 42, He tells them to watch but then turns around and tells them that they do not know what hour He is coming and then equates His return to a thief. How can you watch for a thief?

Unless you are constantly prepared for the thief. That is precisely what Jesus tells them in verse 44 "be ready."

Nevertheless, how are we to be ready? If we do not know when, how can we watch? How do we prepare if we do not know what to look for?

The remaining verses in this chapter may give us some insight into how to be prepared.

> *Who then is a faithful and wise servant, whom his Lord hath made ruler over his household, to give them meat in due season? Blessed is that servant, whom his Lord when he cometh shall find so doing. Verily I say unto you, That he shall make him ruler over all his goods. But and if that evil servant shall say in his heart, My Lord delayeth his coming; And shall begin to smite his fellowservants, and to eat and drink with the drunken; The Lord of that servant shall come in a day when he looketh not for him, and in an hour that he is not aware of, And shall cut him asunder, and appoint him his portion with the hypocrites: there shall be weeping and gnashing of teeth.*
>
> *Matthew 24:45-51 (KJV)*

If you want to be ready, you must fulfill verse 45. The Lord has made us rulers over His household. When he returns, he will be looking for those working on the task assigned to them.

There will be those who are not looking for Him to come. Verse 50 outlines this. These servants are not about the task that has been assigned to them. They are abusing their fellow servants. They are eating and drinking with drunks. Their actions are no different from the world that is around them. These are evil servants.

The faithful servant will be feeding the household of God in their season. The faithful servant did not need to watch for the coming of the Lord because he knew that the Lord could come at any moment. Therefore, the faithful servant took on the task given to him. He performed it with faithfulness until the appearance of the Lord.

The Lord is coming. This fact we know. The key element is not looking for a sign of His return. The critical task is to be about His business when He returns.

We walked many miles in this chapter to return to the Mount of Olive. Jesus began His conversation with the disciples at this location. What takeaway points can we leave this chapter with? What facts are foundationally and scripturally valid?

We know that the "time of Noah," "the time of Lot," and the "time of Jonah" were all used as references to the coming of the Son of Man. We know that a message was given and delivered at each of these events on how to escape the coming judgment. We know that a means of escape was prepared for those who would heed the message. We also see that a gathering of those to be saved occurred.

These facts lead us to one conclusion. The church is the sign for our generation, specifically, the manifestation of the Kingdom of God to the world through the church's actions. We have the message of salvation. We are the way to escape the coming judgment. We cannot waste our time looking for some sign when we are the sign. The time of the gathering together of God's elect is at hand. The church needs to be ready. The church needs to be about the purpose for which God established us to be here.

If the Lord returns and we are sitting in a corner looking through a telescope trying to figure out what the signs in heaven are telling us about the coming of the Lord, and we are not about our father's business seeking to save that which is lost. He will look at us and say, "You slothful and unprofitable servant."

Observing the times and seasons is not bad, but it should not consume all our time and energy because today is the day of salvation. It is high time the church stopped looking for the sign and started being the sign for the modern-day generation of Noah.

God placed supernatural manifestations within the church to show His glory to the world. It is time that signs and wonders manifest in the church so the world can see the church is not just a manmade organization but the gateway through which the Kingdom of Heaven is manifest on the earth.

The manifestation of the true Spirit-filled supernatural church is the sign of Jonah, Lot, and Noah. It is high time the church stands up and becomes the church God called her to be.

The judgment of God is coming to the world. We are not immune to the fulfillment of scripture. The Lord is not delaying His coming. The church needs to be prepared and ready to be the Ark of salvation to this generation.

The rain of revival is beginning to fall. Stories of miracles, signs, and wonders are occurring worldwide. There is no time to waste looking for a sign to tell us to go out into the world and operate in the supernatural. We are the church, not a building but a direct channel through which God will manifest His supernatural power to this world. There is no time to waste this Generation depends on us. We must step outside our ordinary lives of eating, drinking, and giving in marriage and become a supernatural portal through which heaven manifests to this earth.

We must begin to pray for the Kingdom of heaven to come, for His will to be done in earth as it is in heaven. We live in the days of Noah; let's build the Ark.

Finding Grace in the Eyes of the Lord

Chapter Two

Surely he scorns the scorners; but he giveth grace unto the lowly.
Proverbs 3: 34 (KJV)

We talked a lot about the time of Noah in the last chapter. However, we did not identify what made Noah different from his generation. How can we find that same standing before God? How would we impact the generation around us if we walked as Noah?

Let us look at the first mention of Noah's character in the Bible.

> *But Noah found grace in the eyes of the LORD. These are the generations of Noah: Noah was a just man and perfect in his generations, and Noah walked with God.*
> *Genesis 6:8-9 (KJV)*

Three unique qualities define Noah. First, he was a just man. Second, He was perfect in his generation. Third, he walked with God. The summation of these three qualities gave rise to Noah finding grace in the eyes of the Lord.

Many people look at Noah today and think, "What a mighty man of faith. I could never be like that." However, these three qualities set Noah apart from his generation before the Ark was built. Knowing that three simple attributes lead to his entire family's salvation from the devastation unleashed upon the world for the wickedness of all humanity is fantastic. Best of all, it is obtainable for us today.

The first step in finding favor in the eyes of God is to realize and understand the dispensation in which we live. In the time of Noah, men did what was right in their own eyes. During the time of Moses, the law was given to instruct men in the ways of righteousness. Today we live under the reign of the King of Kings in the shadow of the cross with the opportunity to be led by the Spirit of God Himself.

What a remarkable shift in perspective from the time of Noah. Noah lived out the three defining characteristics that allowed him to find grace because he saw it was the right thing to do. Today we as the church have been given the Spirit of God to instruct and guide us daily to live a life that models these three traits. We do not need to rely solely on our opinion of right or wrong. We have the Spirit of God to lead us.

Noah lived righteously according to his own will. Something within Noah gave him a clear understanding of living a just and perfect life walking with God. Not everyone possessed this quality.

This is why Christ came to lay the foundation for all humankind to walk with God in a just and perfect manner.

Understanding that Christ is the definitive cornerstone of this dispensation helps set the stage for living righteously. Because Christ is our example, we can look to Him for answers. We can examine His Word for revelation. We can become perfect in our generation, perfect/mature in our dispensation.

What defines being just?

As we have noted, Noah was a just man. The Hebrew word "just" used to define Noah is צַדִּיק "tsaddiq" which means "just or righteous."

According to the New Testament, "righteousness" is embodied by Jesus. When we read the Gospels, we see the righteousness of God through the works that Jesus did. Nevertheless, how can we obtain the level of righteousness in which Jesus walked?

Simply put, our pathway to righteousness is through Christ.

For he hath made him to be sin for us, who knew no sin; that we might be made the righteousness of God in him.

2 Corinthians 5:21 (KJV)

We all know that we are innately wicked. Without God, our minds are perverse and self-serving. None of us is righteous. Nevertheless, Christ took on our sins so that we could become the righteousness of God. We put on Christ in baptism (Galatians 3:27) through the New Birth (John 3:5, Acts 2: 1-38, 1 Peter 1:3) experience. Through Christ's finished work of the cross and our New Birth, we become the righteousness of God.

Does this mean we can sin and still be righteous? God forbid. Moreover, we are dead to sin, and our new man is alive unto God. We have the opportunity to live a life of righteousness before God. Alternatively, we can choose to sin and separate ourselves again from the will and purpose of God. The choice is ours to make.

The Greek word used in 2 Corinthians 5:21 for righteousness is δικαιοσύνη (dikaiosýnē). This word means "judicial approval." It implies justice, justness, and righteousness. The implications of this Greek word are legal in nature. Today's connotation may not lay a proper foundation for "righteousness."

To understand righteousness, we must look at the modern definition of righteous "acting according to the divine or moral law," and the word origination, from the Old English "rihtwīs," from "riht" 'right' + wīs' manner, state, condition. Wise is the word we derived from the Old English "wīs." The original connotation of righteousness was "right wise."

If we take the original connotation of the word "Righteous" and overlay it with the Greek word used in the scripture. We come to a better understanding of what has been given to us. God has given us the ability to demonstrate judicial approval compared to God's wisdom (right wise).

We make this distinction to understand that God made us His righteousness so we can display the right-wisdom of God.

Having righteousness given to us is meaningless if we do not display the provided righteous nature. Having judicial approval and not showing actions in accordance with the judicial system revokes judicial approval. God is righteous in His nature. God is wise, and His wisdom is perfect and right. It is a fundamental characteristic of who God is. If we are His children and have been made His righteousness, we should display the characteristics that align with His nature. If we have been judicially approved before God, our actions should align with God's judicial system.

Having righteousness without displaying righteous deeds is like owning a Cadillac with a tank full of gas and pushing a rusty bike to work instead of driving the Cadillac. At some point, what you have been giving has to be displayed.

We will briefly mention justification as a side note. Justification is not an internal quality. In the legal sense, Justification is a judgment or evaluation of the actions of someone. If someone's actions align with proper moral standards, they are justified in the eyes of others.

When you use a word processor program like the one used to write and typeset this book, the lines of text have been justified. This means the text on the left and right sides is straight in line with the margins of the page. The margins define the area in which the text resides. It is no longer justified if the text is outside the margins or does not align with the margins.

For something to be just, it must have a standard of comparison. Imagine getting a gallon or a liter of gasoline to understand this better. You know that your gas can will hold precisely 1 gallon. You have a mark on the side of the can that tells you when the can is full. This mark is exactly 1 gallon. For those who measure in liters image, it is a liter mark. You begin putting fuel into the can. You watch the gauge on the pump as it ticks up towards a gallon/liter. You slow it down so you do not overfill the can as it gets close. You slowly fill it until the gauge on the pump is precisely 1 gallon/liter. Then you look at your gas can. However, you only have ¾ of a can of gas.

There is something wrong with the gauge on the pump. You go to tell the gas station owner that there is a problem. He replies that his pump is calibrated precisely to what he thinks a gallon/liter should be. What he thinks a gallon/liter should be is not the standard to which a gallon/liter is defined.

What the gas station owner "feels or believes" is a gallon/liter is irrelevant to what a gallon/liter truly is. A gallon/liter is defined by a standard compared to everything else.

We compare to a standard so that no one is cheated. This standard is used to justify or calibrate the measurement. This standard is a just measure of weight. Righteousness is the moral integrity that ensures you display a just set of behaviors.

> *A false balance is an abomination to the LORD: but a just weight is his delight.*
>
> Proverbs 11:1 (KJV)

Why do we make this demarcation concerning justification versus righteousness? Because we can be made the righteousness of God but not display His righteousness in our actions. When the world sees our actions, we are not justified in their eyes nor in the eyes of God. In truth, our good works should bring glory to God by those who witness them. If our actions do not measure up against the righteousness of God, then we are unjust servants.

> *Ye see then how that by works a man is justified, and not by faith only.*
>
> James 2:24 (KJV)

Noah was just in his generation not simply because he possessed righteousness but because he lived out life before his generation that measured up to God's standard for his generation. Many Christians today may have righteousness within them, but they fail to manifest this righteousness to the world around them. Some say, "How can you have righteousness and not display it?"

> *Therefore to him that knoweth to do good, and doeth it not, to him it is sin.*
>
> *James 4:17 (KJV)*

Many of us know what is good. Sometimes we see people in need and desire to help, but we neglect the opportunity. The nature of God is within us, compelling us to step forth and do what is good, but we quench the Spirit and fail to act upon God's leading.

The enemy will try to flood our minds with excuses and fear. Still, in reality, by failing to respond to the leading of the Spirit within us, we are denying the power of God and failing to display His glory. We must not quench the Spirit. We must reach deep within our new spiritual nature and allow the Spirit of God to quicken our mortal body to become the manifestation of the righteousness of Christ to this generation.

We can see that being "just" in our generation is obtainable. We have the capacity through the New Birth to be "just." We have the Spirit of God to lead us in the paths of righteousness. However, the actual test is found in our actions. Are we living a life that is just before men?

We have taken a long road to get to this point. We have discovered the potential given to us by God through the New Birth. This potential, if released, will lead us to be "just" in this generation.

How can we be perfect? Can we also be perfect in our generation? What are the keys to being perfect in this generation? Is being perfect even obtainable?

To many, the word perfect implies an impossible goal. However, when we look at the scripture, we must understand the Hebrew word used for perfect is תָּמִים (tamim) which means complete or sound. This Hebrew word is very similar to the Greek word used in Ephesians.

> *Till we all come in the unity of the faith, and of the knowledge of the Son of God, unto a perfect man, unto the measure of the stature of the fullness of Christ:*
>
> *Ephesians 4:13 (KJV)*

The Greek word translated as "perfect" in this passage is τέλειος (téleios), which means "perfect, complete, full-grown, mature and lacking nothing." The connotation of téleios is perfection in this context of maturity.

Our goal as Christians is to grow into the full stature of Christ and to become like Him. Our level of maturity defines our perfection. We are not striving to be perfect. We are growing in grace and favor with God towards perfection/maturity. In the process of growth, we become more mature and begin to display the traits of Christ in our lives.

We can only achieve the status of "being perfect in our generation" if we submit to the leading of the Spirit and grow. It is possible to be a mature Christ-like believer. However, we must be willing to put in the effort and grow. Many people believe it is impossible to be like Christ. They think Jesus was the ultimate example, and it is outside our ability to be like Him. So close is good enough. Jesus goes a step further than using Himself as the standard of maturity; He uses God as the mark of perfection/maturity.

> *Be ye therefore perfect, even as your Father which is in heaven is perfect.*
>
> *Matthew 5:48 (KJV)*

If it were not obtainable, then why did Jesus tell His disciples to be perfect even as your Father, which is in heaven, is perfect? The key to understanding "being perfect" comes from the verses that lead up to this statement by Jesus in Matthew.

> *Ye have heard that it hath been said, Thou shalt love thy neighbour, and hate thine enemy.*
> *But I say unto you, Love your enemies, bless them that curse you, do good to them that hate you, and pray for them which despitefully use you, and persecute you;*

> *That ye may be the children of your Father which is in heaven: for he maketh his sun to rise on the evil and on the good, and sendeth rain on the just and on the unjust.*
>
> *For if ye love them which love you, what reward have ye? do not even the publicans the same?*
>
> *And if ye salute your brethren only, what do ye more than others? do not even the publicans so?*
>
> *Be ye therefore perfect, even as your Father which is in heaven is perfect.*
>
> *Matthew 5:43-48 (KJV)*

From the context of this passage, we learn about an aspect of the nature of God. We know that He is not a respecter of persons. He makes it rain on the just and the unjust. Jesus uses this aspect of God's nature to instruct the disciples in the way they should show love. We should not set criteria for who, how, or why we love people around us.

Being perfect and being just go hand in hand. Because we have the righteousness of God, we can act upon this righteous nature towards those around us. We become just in the eyes of those affected by our actions. However, we are imperfect if we display justice towards others based on criteria we define worthy of our actions.

Our just display of righteousness is made perfect when we do good to all men, even as God allows the sun to shine on the evil and the good. We see then this law of righteousness that leads to justification. A law that we walk in not because we are without a choice but a law that is written in our hearts. If we love everyone as we love ourselves and do good to all men everywhere, we fulfill the law of righteousness. Suppose we fulfill this law without prejudice or favoritism. In that case, we can be perfect even as our heavenly Father is perfect.

We must be like God. I hear religious readers declaring that it is sacrilegious to say we can be like God. If it were not obtainable, then why would Jesus have told His disciples to be perfect τέλειος (téleios)? God is τέλειος (téleios). God is our ultimate example of maturity. God made us in His image, and if we are growing into the mature creation God intended us to be, we should start to look like the image of God.

> *So God created man in his own image, in the image of God created he him; male and female created he them.*
>
> *Genesis 1:27 (KJV)*

Once we understand that to be perfect, we must grow into God's image and reflect His glory, and the growth process can genuinely start. When we look at the life of Christ, and the attributes and actions of God described in His Word, we get a clearer picture of who we are created to be. The Word of God is not a book of guidelines to live by. It is a revelation of the nature of God by which we measure our transformation and maturity. The Word of God helps us see our true spiritual nature in light of the image of God. We are transformed into His likeness as we grow in grace and truth as we behold His image.

> *But we all, with open face beholding as in a glass the glory of the Lord, are changed into the same image from glory to glory, even as by the Spirit of the Lord.*
>
> *2 Corinthians 3:28 (KJV)*

The only way for us to become mature is to start growing. The concepts and teaching of spiritual growth and development are not the focus of this book. In truth, the only way to grow is through the leading of the Spirit. Your prayer life, giving, fasting, obedience, and service to the Lord lead us to perfection. The time you spend meditating on God's Word and communing with Him helps you mature. Our interaction with our fellow man helps us develop our Spiritual traits and strengthen our Spiritual nature.

Suppose we are to be perfect in our generation. In that case, we must begin to grow and show forth God's image, nature, and characteristics to this generation.

Being just and perfect in this generation requires each of us to work. It will not come easy. It will require us to exert effort. There will be opposition. The enemy of our soul will fight us every step of the way. However, there is a secret weapon to which we have access that will help guide us. God has given us His Spirit to lead and guide us into all truth.

This brings us to the final trait given to describe Noah. Noah walked with God.

Many people and religions strive to be just and perfect in this world. However, they only succeed in generating a list of rules to govern action but never discover what they seek. They are seeking a formula to make them like God. Inside of us is a desire to fulfill our true spiritual nature. We can never achieve this on our own without God. We need God, not a formula or pattern.

We must walk with God. Noah walked with God. In this dispensation, we have something that Noah did not have. We have the Spirit of God living within us. We are not sure what defined Noah's walk with God. We know that God talked to Noah. The scripture does not define the nature of God's walk with man before the flood. Nevertheless, today we can walk and communicate with God every moment of every day. His Spirit is within us, ever-present, leading us and instructing us.

In this dispensation, we have been given the ability to be just, perfect, and walk with God, just like Noah. But so many people have not discovered this truth. They seek to find favor in the eyes of God through so many other means. However, they fail to look into the scripture to find the true path to God's favor.

Many people seek gifts, or they seek the prestige of a position. They study the various doctrinal nuances of denominations to find respect in knowledge. However, none of these pursuits led to God's favor. We must love mercy, seek justice, and walk humbly with God to find favor in the eyes of God.

Many ministers have risen to high esteem in the eyes of the church. They have exercised their faith and have the gifts of the Spirit in operation in their lives, but they are not just in this generation, nor are they perfect. Their walk with God is lacking in some areas. These areas become stumbling blocks to these ministers, and they fall.

The Lord is looking for a generation, a Noah generation, which will put aside the pursuit of prestige, accolades of men, and gifts. He is looking for a generation to step forth in this lost world, love without favoritism, and do good to all men irrespective of their wickedness. A generation that will listen and obey the leading of the Spirit of God without murmuring or complaining. A generation that will follow God wholeheartedly, even in persecution.

This generation will see the mighty works of the Lord manifest in the land of the living. Not because they were seeking the signs but because they were seeking the God of signs and wonders.

Are you ready to be that generation? Are you willing to lay aside whom you think you want to be or the Christian facade you have taken on and humble yourself in obedience to God? Are you willing to show yourself just before all men, irrespective of who they are or what they do? Are you ready to give perfect love to the sinner and the saint? Are you willing to walk with God by faith without hesitation?

The choice is yours. If you want to find favor in the eyes of God, God has made a way. However, you must take the steps required to earn that favor. The rain is coming. The way of escape from the coming judgment is being constructed. It is time to do your part. What is stopping you?

The Promise of Provision

Chapter Three

But my God shall supply all your need according to his riches in glory by Christ Jesus.
Philippians 4:19 (KJV)

Imagine, if you will, what Noah was thinking when he was tasked with caring for all those animals on an enclosed ship. How was he going to gather them? How was he going to feed them? How long was all this going to take? The list of questions could go on and on.

The answer to all these questions was God. God gave Noah a task, and he had to come through on the provision. For around 364 days, Noah, his family, and all those animals were on the Ark. The only information given to Noah regarding provision was a simple command.

> *And take thou unto thee of all food that is eaten, and thou shalt gather it to thee; and it shall be for food for thee, and for them.*
>
> *Genesis 6:21 (KJV)*

Noah built the Ark. Noah gathered the food. Noah preached the message. God gathered the animals, and Noah loaded them onto the Ark. Noah entered the ship. Then God took over. God shut the door. God made the provision last for 364 days.

The first time God spoke to Noah in Genesis 6:21, Noah was not even given a date or a time frame for when the flood was coming. Noah had no idea how long the food would be stored before the deluge began. Noah was not told how many days they would be on the Ark.

How do you plan when you do not have all the pertinent information to properly prepare?

There was an underlying promise of provision in the middle of all God commanded Noah to do. If Noah believed God and did according to God's commands, God would take care of the rest. Noah could not make it rain. Noah could not make the provision last until the flood ended. Feeding the two elephants that would have been on the Ark would have required a minimum of 145,600 lbs. of food and 36,400 gallons of water. Although it is unknown how many animals were on the Ark, storing the food would have been a massive undertaking. Nevertheless, God provided.

The amount of food Noah had on hand when God gave him the mission to build the Ark did not determine the number of animals brought onto the Ark. The number of trees growing on Noah's farm did not determine the size of the Ark. The command of God determined the number of animals that would be on the Ark and the size of the Ark.

We often allow finances to determine the vision God has given us. In truth, the provision for the vision is in God's hands. Our participation in God's vision is one of faith. The resources God gives us are to accomplish God's vision for our life. If we are not working to achieve God's vision, we should not complain when we lack provision. It is called pro-vision; provision is needed to manifest the vision. The prefix "pro" means "for."

So many times, we are crippled by what we see concerning the resources at hand. Lack prevents us from stepping out on faith and following God's vision. In truth, we are to walk by faith and not by sight.

Our wealth, prosperity, or resources level is not tallied into God's calling on our life. The only resource we need is God. The provision is within His hand if we seek His calling and purpose.

> *The young lions do lack, and suffer hunger: but they that seek the LORD shall not want any good thing.*
>
> *Psalms 34:10 (KJV)*

Look at the church from the standpoint of the Ark for a moment. The church is being built not by man but by God. He is the one who laid the foundation. He is the one who joins the pieces together. He places each person in particular to serve a distinct role within the church. Without God, the church would not even exist.

The true church comprises people who have been moved upon by the Spirit of God. The drawing of the Spirit leads to a relationship with God. This relationship leads to repentance and begins the process of being born again into the family of God. Man himself cannot build the church.

Each of us is a minister of the church with our own gifts and callings. We are not builders. We are the construction materials. One of our roles is to sow the seed that will draw men into a relationship with God.

Our role as servants/leaders in the Kingdom of God affords us great privilege but does not make us the builder.

> *Now therefore ye are no more strangers and foreigners, but fellowcitizens with the saints, and of the household of God; And are built upon the foundation of the apostles and prophets, Jesus Christ himself being the chief corner stone; In whom all the building fitly framed together groweth unto an holy temple in the Lord: In whom ye also are builded together for an habitation of God through the Spirit.*
>
> *Ephesians 2: 19-22 (KJV)*

As the church, we are the Ark, God's habitation. We are the storehouse in which the Lord places His provision. The resources the Lord puts in our care are what the Lord has gathered into the Ark for provision. A minister once said, "If the church members would give what they have and distribute it to the needs of the saints, there would be no lack in the church."

The Lord has given us the time needed to fulfill His plan and purpose. God has placed in His church the provision required to manifest His vision. The key to success is not seeking more time and resources. The key is maximizing those resources to fulfill the Kingdom's purpose.

People pray for God to pour out more power into the church. They act powerless and can do nothing until God gives them more power. However, He has already given us all power and authority in Heaven and the Earth.

> *And Jesus came and spake unto them, saying, All power is given unto me in heaven and in earth. Go ye therefore, and teach all nations, baptizing them in the name of the Father, and of the Son, and of the Holy Ghost: Teaching them to observe all things whatsoever I have commanded you: and, lo, I am with you alway, even unto the end of the world. Amen.*
>
> *Matthew 28:18-20 (KJV)*

Jesus was given all the power of heaven and earth, then He turned to His disciples and gave them the commission to use His name. There are many instances in the scripture where the name of

Jesus is used to cast out devils, heal the sick, and baptize people. In addition, we are commanded to do everything in the name of Jesus Colossians 3:17.

To truly understand what this means, we must look beyond our current understanding of the English word for "name" and look at the Greek word used in the scriptures. The Greek word used in the scripture for "name" is ὄνομα (ónoma). This word not only means name but also authority or cause. To do an activity in the ónoma of another person is to act as a manifestation or representative of someone's character or power of attorney. From the connotation of Hebrew tradition, a name is inseparable from the person to whom it belongs, and it contains something of a person's essence.

When Jesus commanded His disciples to do things in His name, He was telling them to act not only as His representatives but to operate in His authority and power. Suppose all power is given to Jesus, who gave us the potential to operate under His authority. What power is left to give if we have all power in heaven and earth at our disposal through His name?

We must understand God is the God of provision. He provides what is needed. Often, what is required to accomplish the vision is in the hands of someone close to the visionary. The critical component is getting the person who holds the provision to open their hand to release the provision to accomplish its purpose. God works on the hearts of those who have so they can support those who are working to manifest God's vision.

We must understand one key concept about God's character to better grasp this flow of resources. We all know the passage of scripture God is love.

He that loveth not knoweth not God; for God is love.
1 John 4:8 (KJV)

The critical key to understanding God is understanding love. In Hebrew, the word for "love" is אהבה (ahava), which is made up of three basic Hebrew letters: aleph (א), hey (ה), and vet (ב). If we break this word down, these three letters are made of two root words. The two letters hey (ה) and vet (ב) make up the root word "hav," which means to give. The letter aleph (א) modifies this word to mean "I give." The very nature of God is to give Himself.

God's desire is not to simply give you what you need. He wants to give through you. He desires to give you the Kingdom but not for you alone. He wants to give you the Kingdom so He can manifest the Kingdom through you. If you have been given oversight of positions in this present world, it is not simply for your benefit. God has given to you so He can give it through you. He desires each of us to become a conduit through which He pours out His love, blessings, and provision.

If you desire the promise of God's provision, you must step up to the task of manifesting God's vision. Each of us has a calling in our lives. We have an expected end that God set for each day of our life. God does have an end goal for our lives, but it is achieved daily. We cannot wait until the provision is in place to work toward the calling. We must begin now.

The Ark was not built when Noah had all the lumber and materials delivered to his front door miraculously by the hand of God. Noah did not begin to lay up food when it appeared in baskets at the entrance of the Ark. He began one step at a time, working towards the end goal God had set for him. When the time came for the flood, Noah's efforts had worked together to provide the starting materials for God to do the rest.

We live in a world that is looking for possessions to define them. Materialism is a primary motivational force. They look for identity in their job. They try to achieve a level of status in the community. They are consumed with a drive to fill a void they cannot fill. They know there has to be more to life, but no road they take leads to fulfillment.

God has a plan for each of our lives, a unique calling, and a purpose that we are to achieve. Inside each of us, we know this fact. Something motivates us to greatness from an early age, a drive that compels us to reach beyond ourselves. However, we will fail if we lack a vision of our destiny. The scripture declares this truth.

Where there is no vision, the people perish: but he that keepeth the law, happy is he.

Proverbs 29:18 (KJV)

Many people reading this book may know this fact. Still, some have forgotten, lost sight of the vision, or have never discovered the purpose for which God ordained their life. To all of these people, let me be frank, it is time to throw everything to the sideline, get on your face before God, and seek His purpose for your life. There is nothing else in this world that will give your life meaning. Accept the purpose for which God has called you.

We can work every day to provide for our needs. We can build the most significant wealth in the world. At the end of our days, when the view of eternity is close, the biggest question on our mind will be, "Did I make a difference?" Eternity is a long time to live with regret. Today is the day to lay up an investment in your eternal reward.

We must use the limited time we have been given to achieve our life's purpose. If we do not accomplish it, no one else will. No one can take our God-given calling. We can sit around waiting for the door to open up for us. We can live life without a vision or step out into our callings.

The problem with many is they are waiting for God to provide the provision. His Word holds many promises regarding His provision.

But My God shall supply all your needs according to His riches in glory in Christ Jesus.

Philippians 4:19 (KJV)

For the Lord God is a sun and shield: the Lord will give grace and glory: no good thing will he withhold from them that walk uprightly.

Psalms 84:11 (KJV)

And we know that all things work together for good to those who love God, to those who are the called according to His purpose.

Romans 8:28 (KJV)

Whatever promises you hold on to, they all come with a prerequisite. You must be called according to His purpose.

The provision for the vision is provided in the process. In other words, the resources we need will only become available when we begin to work towards achieving the vision. We cannot wait for the provision to begin. Begin, and the provision will become available. So many people wait for the provision before they start working for God. He has it in place if we would just take the first steps. That should be so motivating!

When Abraham took his son Isaac to the top of Mount Moriah, he took the wood for the fire and a knife for the sacrifice. Isaac asked him about the sacrifice. To which Abraham replied, "God will provide Himself a sacrifice." The prophetic meaning of this is apparent. However, the provision is rarely noticed.

If Abraham had waited on God to provide the sacrifice at the foot of Mount Moriah, he would never have found the provision. The provision did not appear until Abraham took up the task of preparation, progression, and pursuit. The ram caught in the thicket was there when Abraham needed the sacrifice. He would not have found the ram in any other location. In the exact place where Abraham required the provision, God had provided what was needed.

Too many times, we do not do what we can do to set the stage for God to do what only He can do. God puts in our hands seeds to sow, but He provides the increase. If we do not plant what we have in our hands, we cannot expect the increase at the hands of God. It is God who provides seed for the sower. If we are not planting what we have, we cannot expect Him to provide an increase.

The promise of provision can manifest in multiple ways. It can be financial, or in many cases, in ways, we do not expect. God may orchestrate the opportunity to meet others who can help propel us into our destiny. There may be times He provides food, shelter, rest, and other times that He provides miracles and wonders. The provision of God is in His hand and by His design. However, we must be present to receive the provision.

If we are off seeking our own path and not the way of the Lord, we may miss the very moment God opens a door for us to step into our ministry. For example, we can pray for God to give us the gift of working miracles. We can desire to lay hands on the sick, who are instantly healed, or raise the dead. However, if we spend all our time locked up in a room or a church pew waiting for the Lord to give it to us, it will likely not manifest.

- How can you see the dead raised if you never pray for a dead person?
- How will you see the blinded eyes open if you never command the eyes of the blind to open?
- How will you ever experience lame walking if you never take the hand of a crippled person and their feet and ankles receive strength?

The Lord has provided ample opportunities for healing all around us. Still, we fail to take His provision and act upon it. If you want to see the glory of God, you have to provide an opportunity for Him to manifest His Glory.

As the prophet Elijah was on Mount Carmel and called all the prophets of Baal together, he created an opportunity for God to show off. He created an environment where God could answer by fire. Are you creating an environment where God can answer by fire? Are you setting the stage for the rain of God to saturate the lives of those around you?

The provision of God is all around us daily. It is time we stop waiting for the provision to arrive and start setting the stage for it to manifest. It is time to prepare for the rain to fall.

The Protection of the Sons

Chapter Four

Children's children are the crown of old men; and the glory of children [are] their fathers.
Proverbs 17: 6 (KJV)

Noah was given a great responsibility. The fate of humanity rested upon his shoulders. He had found grace in the eyes of the Lord and was "perfect and just" in his generation. He walked with the Lord. This set the stage for God to speak with him and give him a plan for escaping the judgment to come. However, what good would one man be in saving the human race? How could humanity re-emerge on this planet without a female to bear children?

The future of mankind was contingent not just on Noah but on his children. God's salvation is not unilateral. God is generational.

In a prior chapter, we addressed how Noah was "just and perfect" in his generation. There is some indication that this was also an indication of the purity of Noah's lineage, given the intermingling of the sons of God and the daughters of men. God's desire to have a righteous lineage with a pure bloodline from Adam through which Jesus could be born may have played a pivotal role in Noah's selection and the desire to save a lineage from Noah's posterity.

> *But with thee will I establish my covenant; and thou shalt come into the Ark, thou, and thy sons, and thy wife, and thy sons' wives with thee. And of every living thing of all flesh, two of every [sort] shalt thou bring into the Ark, to keep [them] alive with thee; they shall be male and female.*
>
> *Genesis 6:18 (KJV)*

Can you imagine what Noah would have thought if God had told him, "Noah, I will destroy the earth. However, I need you to make an Ark to save the animals and yourself. Say goodbye to your family. I am going to destroy them all?" That would have been devastating. Why would Noah even have built the Ark? To work all those years just to watch your family die. His feeling of emotional loss would have sealed the fate of mankind and all animals. How could you even build something you know would leave you alone with the memories of the death of all those you loved? What motivation would Noah have had to even begin construction?

For the preservation of mankind, the establishment of Noah's legacy, and for the glory of God to be manifest to all generations, God had to protect the sons of Noah. Not only the son but also their wives.

When you look at the events following the flood, everyone left alive could only testify that their entire existence was the direct result of God. God is all about displaying His glory. As the days unfold, we must keep this distinct principle in mind. Even though we are each unique in our own right, at the end of our days, God's only desire for us is that our lives bring Him glory.

That may sound selfish, but we must know what glory truly is to understand this principle. The Hebrew word כָּבוֹד (kabod) and the Greek word δοξα (doxa) are translated as glory in the Scriptures. These words imply "weight, heaviness, judgment, opinion," and by extension, "good reputation, honor." The Scriptures even state that Jesus manifested glory through His works.

> *This beginning of miracles did Jesus in Cana of Galilee, and manifested forth his glory; and his disciples believed on him.*
> *John 2:11 (KJV)*

Jesus even tells his disciples that God's glory will manifest when people see their good works.

> *Let your light so shine before men, that they may see your good works, and glorify your Father which is in heaven.*
> *Matthew 5:16 (KJV)*

I must take an aside here and explain what I mean by the manifestation of God's glory. When a person is without the knowledge of God nor acknowledges God or His existence. God is not esteemed or enthroned in His proper place in creation. However, those who do not retain God in their knowledge face the fact that God must exist. The things they have seen and heard could not be accurate in the natural unless a supernatural event occurred. That person is left with no other option but to acknowledge the existence of God.

This brings us to the word used in this passage of scripture which is translated as "glorify." The Greek word is δοξάζω (doxazó) which means to bestow "doxa" (glory) onto something. This word is a verb of action. When a person glorifies God, they personally acknowledge God for His true character or the manifestation of His image. In other words, they are acknowledging the weight of the evidence before them concerning the existence of God.

How does this equate to the protection of sons, you might ask? We would have to start at the beginning to understand this concept. We know that man was created in the image of God. We know that God breathed the breath of life into man, and he became a living soul. Therefore, in all creation, only one created being can fully display the characteristics of God.

And God said, Let us make man in our image, after our likeness: and let them have dominion over the fish of the sea,

> *and over the fowl of the air, and over the cattle, and over all the earth, and over every creeping thing that creepeth upon the earth.*
>
> *Genesis 1:26 (KJV)*

Man was created to be the express image of God's nature in this world. However, the man fell. The serpent's deception to take a shortcut to become like God created separation from the God who created man.

In all his sin, man still possessed a remnant of Godly traits. The conscience of man is a residue of his original spiritual nature. God could have utterly destroyed mankind from the face of the earth. However, something within man was of value to God.

God's plan from the foundation of the world was to redeem man if he fell. Noah was a proxy for the salvation of mankind. The sons of Noah were the vestige from which complete salvation would be birthed.

Why, you might ask? Because God desires His glory to be manifest throughout all creation. For some reason, God selected mankind to display His glory to the unseen rulers in heavenly places.

> *And to make all men see what is the fellowship of the mystery, which from the beginning of the world hath been hid in God, who created all things by Jesus Christ: To the intent that now unto the principalities and powers in heavenly places might be*

> *known by the church the manifold wisdom of God, According to the eternal purpose which he purposed in Christ Jesus our Lord:*
>
> *Ephesians 3:9-11 (KJV)*

Let us begin to unpack this by looking at the events that established the dispensation in which we now live. After the death, burial, and resurrection of Jesus Christ, the disciples were sent to Jerusalem to tarry until they were endued with power from on high.

> *And, behold, I send the promise of my Father upon you: but tarry ye in the city of Jerusalem, until ye be endued with power from on high.*
>
> *Luke 24:49 (KJV)*

What was this power? Many people say it was the power to heal the sick, cast out devils, and do the works Jesus did. However, further analysis of the scriptures reveals that this power was already given to the disciples (Luke 10: 1-24, Mark 6:7-12).

Some would say it is the power to speak in other tongues, but this is defined as a gift or a sign, not a "power" throughout the scriptures. Scripture supports the manifestation of speaking in unknown tongues accompanying the baptism/being filled with the Holy Ghost. This gift/sign is available to all who desire to receive it. The Holy Ghost gives the ability to speak in an unknown tongue.

But the "power" endowed by the baptism of the Holy Ghost was not speaking in tongues, albeit it is a sign of the infilling of the Spirit.

The distinguishing quality associated with the outpouring of the Holy Ghost on the day of Pentecost was far greater. The promise of the indwelling of the Holy Ghost gave access to the Kingdom of God. Let us look at a scripture that will give us insight into our discussion.

> *But as many as received him, to them gave he power to become the sons of God, even to them that believe on his name: Which were born, not of blood, nor of the will of the flesh, nor of the will of man, but of God.*
>
> *John 1:12-13 (KJV)*

The day of Pentecost opened a doorway for us to become a part of the family of God by giving mankind the power to become the Sons of God.

You may ask why the power to become a Son of God is necessary to understand the dispensation we live in, you may ask? God is a God of family.

- He saved Noah's family because of Noah's uprightness.
- He blesses Abraham's descendants because of Abraham's faithfulness.

- He promised the Messiah through David's lineage because of David's heart.

It only makes logical sense that our dispensation is built upon Sonship within the family of God.

All creation is waiting for this concept to manifest in the church. Creation is waiting for the children of God to mature into the position Christ left for them to fill. Creation is waiting for the mature Sons of God to step into their position of authority.

> *For the earnest expectation of the creature waiteth for the manifestation of the sons of God. For the creature was made subject to vanity, not willingly, but by reason of him who hath subjected the same in hope, Because the creature itself also shall be delivered from the bondage of corruption into the glorious liberty of the children of God. For we know that the whole creation groaneth and travaileth in pain together until now.*
>
> *Romans 8:19-22 (KJV)*

The sons and, by extension, the daughters of God make up the church of the living God, the true church, the body of Christ, and the Kingdom of God. God is building the church to save and redeem His children. The church is for the protection of the sons.

> *Behold, what manner of love the Father hath bestowed upon us, that we should be called the sons of God: therefore the world*

> *knoweth us not, because it knew him not. Beloved, now are we the sons of God, and it doth not yet appear what we shall be: but we know that, when he shall appear, we shall be like him; for we shall see him as he is. And every man that hath this hope in him purifieth himself, even as he is pure.*
>
> 1 John 3:1-3 (KJV)

I can hear the gears grinding in the minds of the theologians reading these words. I assure you the focus of God's plan for redemption was to bring us into the family of God. We can only become sons by birth, and the New Birth experience, as manifest on the day of Pentecost, ushered in the dispensation of the sonship of man back into the family of God.

We have now arrived at an essential juncture in our walk with God. In truth, many have approached salvation as a ticket out of hell. This was never God's intention. The reward of the righteous is eternity with God, but the salvation of mankind was never about the reward it was about the job the sons were to accomplish.

In the case of Noah, the sons were included in the plan of salvation to build the Ark, gather the food, and ensure they and their wives were onboard at the time of the door closing. There were very specific tasks that the sons needed to perform. In the absence of these tasks, being completed the Ark and the subsequent salvation of mankind was at risk. Once the Ark doors opened after the flood, the salvation of mankind was again placed upon the sons of Noah.

They had to produce offspring for the hope of mankind's redemption to be manifest.

Just because we come to Jesus and are born again does not remove us from the work that needs to be accomplished. In truth, it puts the burden of the work of God for the salvation of mankind in our hands. Our task is to labor and work to display the glory of God around us so that the world can see our works and glorify our Father in Heaven.

This is a great place to be because God desires to show Himself through supernatural manifestation. When nature comes into alignment with the presence of God, the supernatural will happen. As it says in the passage above (1 John 3:3), the key is for us to be pure. It is not about our agenda. It is about God's glory. We must be true, and we must walk in grace.

And the Word was made flesh, and dwelt among us, (and we beheld his glory, the glory as of the only begotten of the Father,) full of grace and truth.

John 1:14 (KJV)

As this passage indicates, the manifestation of the glory of God will be full of grace and truth. It is not time to build our own name and ministry for ourselves. As it was in the days of Noah, it was not about making a reputation for Noah. I am sure that many people thought Noah had lost his mind. The work placed in Noah's hands was for the salvation of man and the manifestation of God's glory. Noah was not building a ministry or a name for himself.

Today God wants to display His glory to the world. He desires signs and wonders to follow those that believe. God wants us to make His name known to all the world just as He appeared to the children of Israel on Mount Sinai so they would know the fear of the Lord and reverence His commandments.

> *And all the people saw the thunderings, and the lightnings, and the noise of the trumpet, and the mountain smoking: and when the people saw it, they removed, and stood afar off. And they said unto Moses, Speak thou with us, and we will hear: but let not God speak with us, lest we die. And Moses said unto the people, Fear not: for God is come to prove you, and that his fear may be before your faces, that ye sin not.*
>
> *Exodus 20:18-20 (KJV)*

God desired to speak with Israel personally. However, they choose to have God speak directly with Moses. God wants to talk with us individually to make His glory and presence known. He expects us to take our position as sons. He wants us to stand before His presence and walk in this world to represent His image and glory.

Today, we have been called, given the power to become, and made the sons of God. As sons, we have a great responsibility placed in our hands. We must show forth the glory of Him who called us.

> *But ye are a chosen generation, a royal priesthood, an holy nation, a peculiar people; that ye should shew forth the praises of him who hath called you out of darkness into his marvellous light:*
>
> *1 Peter 2:9 (KJV)*

The church is the sign for this generation that the favor of God is upon us. He has laid up for us provision to accomplish His vision, and He will protect His children. However, we must be about our Father's business. We must begin showing forth the Glory of God with signs and wonders.

We have spent centuries as the church trying to define and refine our doctrines. Still, Paul knew what truly distinguished the church of the living God was not the enticing words of man or the words of the wise but the demonstration of the power of God.

> *And my speech and my preaching was not with enticing words of man's wisdom, but in demonstration of the Spirit and of power: That your faith should not stand in the wisdom of men, but in the power of God.*
>
> *1 Corinthians 2:4-5 (KJV)*

The earth is groaning for the sons of God to stand up and display the power of God. We must make disciples of all men. This is true. However, in-depth theological indoctrination is not the beginning of discipleship. Discipleship begins in the manifestation of His glory by demonstrating the Spirit and of power.

> *This beginning of miracles did Jesus in Cana of Galilee, and manifested forth his glory; and his disciples believed on him.*
> *John 2:11 (KJV)*

God has promised that He would protect His sons. Now He left in our hands the task of gathering His children into the Ark of safety, the church. He placed within us His power, His Spirit, His mercy, and His grace for us to show forth His glory to the world around us. It is time that we step into our role as sons and demonstrate the power of the Spirit by manifesting the gifts in operation, with signs and wonders following. It is time we become the church, the actual expression of the body of Christ.

The Plan Is Given

Chapter Five

This is the purpose that is purposed upon the whole earth: and this is the hand that is stretched out upon all the nations.
Isaiah 14:26 (KJV)

God is not without a plan. As humans, we cannot see the grand design. We know that we have a part to play in His masterpiece. As Noah found out, God intended him to work to accomplish His plan. He will give us the blueprints, but we must participate in the endeavor. No one else can fulfill our role. If Noah had not done his part, there would have been no one to take his place.

Make thee an ark of gopher wood; rooms shalt thou make in the Ark, and shalt pitch it within and without with pitch. And this is the fashion which thou shalt make it of: The length of the Ark shall be three hundred cubits, the breadth of it fifty cubits, and the height of it thirty cubits. A window shalt thou make to the Ark, and in a cubit shalt thou finish it above; and the door of the ark shalt thou set in the side thereof; with lower, second, and third stories shalt thou make it.

Genesis 6:14 (KJV)

And of every living thing of all flesh, two of every sort shalt thou bring into the Ark, to keep them alive with thee; they shall be male and female. Of fowls after their kind, and of cattle after their kind, of every creeping thing of the earth after his kind, two of every sort shall come unto thee, to keep them alive. And take thou unto thee of all food that is eaten, and thou shalt gather it to thee; and it shall be for food for thee, and for them. Thus did Noah; according to all that God commanded him, so did he.

Genesis 6:19-22 (KJV)

God was not going to build the Ark. God desired Noah to be a co-laborer with Him in the process of salvation. There were three things that Noah was responsible for doing. Number one, it was Noah's responsibility to build the ark. Number two, Noah's responsibility was to place the animals on the ark. Number three, Noah's responsibility was to gather the food onto the ark.

When we consider these three tasks, we quickly see that none of these tasks was outside the realm of possibility for Noah to perform. Some of them may have taken more effort, but Noah was well able to play his part. God did not ask Noah to make the flood occur or make it rain. God required Noah to do what he could accomplish, and God would do the rest.

Mark Batterson once said, "If your dream does not scare you, it is too small." I will add to that statement the following. "If your dream can be achieved through natural means, it is not a God dream." You may ask yourself, if Noah was given a task that he could perform, was his dream too small?

We must understand that Noah's task was not the vision or dream God gave him. The vision God gave Noah was the salvation of mankind.

While Noah began gathering the building materials and constructing the Ark, I am sure the people asked him what he was doing. I would say he asked himself many times, "What am I doing?" No matter what the answer was, he continued to construct the ark. The vision to build the ark was well within the possibility for Noah, but the flood was beyond his comprehension.

The vision Noah had was not of the ark. The vision was of the flood. All Noah could do was follow the plan and build the ark. Every board, fastener, and tar patching was the direct result of the vision of the destruction to come and the promised salvation through his obedience. When Noah worked on the ark, he did not see the structure. He saw a means of escape. It made no logical sense to those looking at what he was building. They could not see the necessity that was laid upon him.

The action of Noah seemed purposeless without the context of the flood. Noah knew that God would bring the rain and flood, so Noah built.

Now is laid upon us the same necessity. A lost world needs our efforts to show them the way to escape from the coming destruction. Our actions may appear foolish to the world, but we have a vantage point they do not have. We see the world from the vantage point of being seated in heavenly places with Christ. We see the coming judgment and the hope of salvation.

Just knowing that destruction is coming is of no help to a lost world. We must understand what our part is to play in the salvation of souls. We must know what the plan is.

What is the plan? How can we achieve the task laid upon us if we do not know what the task is? We must look to the Scripture to find the plan. We see the vision/will of God is that no one should perish but that all should come to repentance. We must now determine our role in achieving this vision.

Uncovering our part in God's plan will require evaluating the commandments given to the early church by Jesus. We begin this quest by looking into the passage of scripture known to many as the "Great Commission."

> *Go ye therefore, and teach all nations, baptizing them in the name of the Father, and of the Son, and of the Holy Ghost: Teaching them to observe all things whatsoever I have*

> *commanded you: and, lo, I am with you alway, even unto the end of the world. Amen.*
>
> *Matthew 28:19-20 (KJV)*

As we read this passage, we can see three tasks assigned to the church.

- Number one, they were to teach all nations.
- Number two, they were to baptize those they taught.
- Number three, they were to teach them to observe what Jesus commanded them.

This is within the realm of possibility. We are capable of achieving these specific tasks. However, we must also look at the things that Christ commanded and observe these. There is a similar passage to this commission in Mark.

> *And he said unto them, Go ye into all the world, and preach the gospel to every creature. He that believeth and is baptized shall be saved; but he that believeth not shall be damned. And these signs shall follow them that believe; In my name shall they cast out devils; they shall speak with new tongues; They shall take up serpents; and if they drink any deadly thing, it shall not hurt them; they shall lay hands on the sick, and they shall recover.*
>
> *Mark 16:15-18 (KJV)*

According to this passage, the concept of baptism is reiterated. However, there are additional tasks given. They are as follows, go into all the world, preach the gospel to every creature, cast out devils, speak in new tongues, take up serpents, drink deadly things, and lay hands on the sick.

For the sake of discussion, we will leave taking up serpents and drinking deadly things in the context of a promise of protection in the event it occurred. Certain sects of the Christian faith practice these things. However, to address this topic, we will simply use Jesus's reply when he was tempted, "Thou shalt not tempt the Lord thy God." For the simplicity of the Gospel, we will not advocate these as tasks that must be performed only as promises of protection.

Let's look at the other task commanded in this passage. Now we are getting into some things that we, in our flesh, cannot achieve without supernatural ability. Healing the sick, casting out devils, and being supernaturally protected from harm. These are outside our ability to do, yet they were commands for us to follow. There has to be more to the story. Looking into the Gospel of Luke, we find a promise given to those early believers.

> *And that repentance and remission of sins should be preached in his name among all nations, beginning at Jerusalem. And ye are witnesses of these things. And, behold, I send the*

> *promise of my Father upon you: but tarry ye in the city of Jerusalem, until ye be endued with power from on high.*
>
> *Luke 24:47-49 (KJV)*

In the context of this passage, we see that Jesus once again lays out a set of tasks for the early church to achieve. These tasks align with the task outline in Matthew and Mark. These tasks include preaching, repentance, remission of sins, and being a witness. However, a promise is given that power would be endued from on high. We will talk more about this shortly. Let us focus on the task as we look into the book of John.

> *Jesus, therefore, said to them again, 'Peace to you; according as the Father hath sent me, I also send you;' and this having said, he breathed on them, and saith to them, 'Receive the Holy Spirit; if of any ye may loose the sins, they are loosed to them; if of any ye may retain, they have been retained.'*
>
> *John 20:21-23 (KJV)*

Jesus speaks of the church being sent as He was sent into the world. He also mentions receiving the Holy Ghost, the promise mentioned in Mark. The tasks given to the church in this passage of scripture are to lose or retain another person's sins. That statement in and of itself would cause ripples in many theological dogmas. For the sake of this chapter, we will not fight those theological debates.

We will just take those tasks as assignments from the Lord. After evaluating one last passage of scripture in Acts, we will list all these tasks.

> *And, being assembled together with them, commanded them that they should not depart from Jerusalem, but wait for the promise of the Father, which, saith he, ye have heard of me. For John truly baptized with water; but ye shall be baptized with the Holy Ghost not many days hence.*
>
> *Acts 1:4-5 (KJV)*

> *But ye shall receive power, after that the Holy Ghost is come upon you: and ye shall be witnesses unto me both in Jerusalem, and in all Judaea, and in Samaria, and unto the uttermost part of the earth.*
>
> *Acts 1:8 (KJV)*

Christ's final task to the early church was to wait for the promise of the Holy Ghost. This promise would provide them with the power that would be required to fulfill the tasks that had been assigned to them. The additional charge that was given to them was to be witnesses.

To recap the tasks given to the early church; Wait for the promise of the Holy Ghost, teach, baptize, preach (gospel, repentance, and remission of sins), observe all the commandments of Christ, go into all the world, cast out devils, speak in new tongues, lay hands on the sick, lose or retain sins of another person, and be witnesses.

We have already reached a point where these tasks seem out of context with today's view of Christianity. This is not the picture of the modern church. Many of these tasks are not even part of the culture of a modern church. However, these are the tasks handed out by Jesus to the early church.

Some of you are saying, "Most of these passages were spoken to the disciples." My question is, "Are we, not all called to be Disciples of Christ?" We must not dismiss our assignment and relegate it to a prior generation. If we do so, we are left with no plan and, subsequently, no purpose.

If we want the results of the scripture, we must take on the responsibility of the scripture. We cannot delegate the responsibility of performing these tasks in our society to a group of men that followed Christ over 2000 years ago and who are now dead. No disrespect, but the disciples performed these tasks during their lifetime to their generation, not our generation. It is time we take up the task for this generation.

As these scripture passages point out, it all begins with receiving the gift of the Holy Ghost and the power associated with that promise. The question is, "Have you received the Holy Ghost since you have believed?"

If not, before you read any further, I adjure you to seek the presence of God and ask to receive the infilling of the Holy Ghost. Jesus said,

> *If ye then, being evil, know how to give good gifts unto your children: how much more shall your heavenly Father give the Holy Spirit to them that ask him?*
>
> *Luke 11:13 (KJV)*

Before you can be equipped to fulfill the tasks Christ left for you to perform, you must be, and you have to be, filled with the Holy Ghost and power.

The power was not to lay hands on the sick, and they recover. As we presented in the last chapter, the power was to become the sons of God. Why is this distinction important? If we receive the power to heal the sick, we will perform works out of our ability. This ability would have been given to us by God. But because we would be performing works, we could then boast. However, if the power was to be a son, we would depend on our Father to lead us and teach us how to operate as a son.

To explain this more effectively, let me provide an anecdotal analogy. For example, imagine you wake up tomorrow with superhuman abilities. You can fly. You can lift 1000 times your weight. You are bulletproof. You can move faster than light. What would you do?

Most people would say, "I would help others." I beg to differ. This may be how it starts, but the power will go to your head before long. You will begin to find things you disagree with, and then you will step in and impose your will in the situation. Some of these may be of great humanitarian concern. Others may just be differences in viewpoints. Nevertheless, before long, everything that is not in accordance with your personal worldview will be changed to match your worldview, to the good or the bad.

There will be those who hail you as a god and others who call you a monster. Left to your own moral compass, not everything will be correct. Nevertheless, who can stop you? You are an invincible, all-powerful dictator of the world. Can you see how this is not the optimal way to obtain power?

Now let us take this from the Scriptural perspective. God wants to manifest His glory to the world through you. He wants people to glorify Him when they see your good works. God desires you to be His child and the workmanship of His hand. He wants you to fulfill your original intent and purpose, which was to be the image of God. To this end, to re-establish the dominion given to Adam in the garden. So God became the way and made a way for you to once again become a son of God and show forth His image.

We have been given the power to become a son of God. He placed apostles, prophets, evangelists, pastors, and teachers in His church to perfect the saints. This passage of scripture from Ephesians distinctly tells us the end results of this process.

> *Till we all come in the unity of the faith, and of the knowledge of the Son of God, unto a perfect man, unto the measure of the stature of the fulness of Christ:*
>
> Ephesians 4:13 (KJV)

The full stature of Christ, what an exciting goal. The purpose of the ministerial process is to make us look like Christ. To make us look like a mature Son of God. This is a deep topic. All the power in the world could be given to us and never make us like Christ. Instead of God giving us all the power in the world, He allows us to become like Christ. Then He gave us His name and authority so that all power in heaven and earth would be at our disposal as we are submitted to God.

Jesus was under subjection to God. He only did what he saw the father doing. We must understand the power that God has given us is not for our own purposes but for His plan to be fulfilled. If we submit ourselves to Him as obedient sons, we have access to all the power of heaven and earth.

The difference rests within the nature of the person using the power. If we access the power of heaven and earth from a fallen state, we will employ this power from the wickedness of our hearts to fulfill our own lustful desires. However, suppose our heart is converted and fashioned not after the carnal nature of fallen man but after the nature of God. In that case, we can employ the power of heaven and earth to manifest the Glory of God.

God's heart for humanity is one of love, not desire. God's passion for man is not to be a selfish dictator but to have fellowship with man. God's plan for man is one of eternal purpose, not temporal gain. Becoming a son of God is the only way to access the power of eternity. This is why many people search for the power of God to manifest in their lives and never find it. They are searching for power and not the God of all power.

As we look at the list of tasks outlined in the scripture by Christ to the church's early leaders, some could be accomplished by natural means, and others could only occur through supernatural power. Let us view each task as a natural versus a supernatural approach.

The first task on our list was to "wait for the promise of the Holy Ghost." Waiting can be done easily in the natural realm. Many people are sitting around waiting even as they read this book. However, I am convinced the early church was not just sitting in a chair waiting for something to happen. If you read the Book of Acts, chapters 1 and 2, you find they were taking care of some church business and praying.

Many times people in the church misunderstand the meaning of the word wait. When you go to a restaurant, someone comes to the table to "wait" on you. They are not sitting in the seat while you take your time to go to the table. They are actively engaged in assisting you in fulfilling your purpose in coming to the restaurant. The same is true with God and the actions of these early church leaders. They had come to Jerusalem and were actively seeking the manifestation of the Holy Ghost that was promised to them.

The act of "waiting" was natural, but the Holy Ghost's outpouring was supernatural. There is no possible way the events of the Day of Pentecost in the Book of Acts could have occurred without a supernatural manifestation of God's Spirit. Given that every task Christ gave was contingent upon this event, it is hard to fathom that someone could perform the remaining task without the Holy Ghost. Nevertheless, let us continue our evaluation of the tasks given to the early church.

The task of "teaching" is next on our list. From the natural perspective, teaching is a normal event in the life of people. We must teach our children. We have specific subjects that are taught in school. Teaching has become so common in the natural world that there are classes taught at universities on how to teach. They have developed different teaching philosophies and approaches. However, from the supernatural standpoint, how can you teach anything? The very laws of nature define the depth and breadth of our knowledge and understanding. We teach from what we know. How can we teach the supernatural if we do not know the supernatural? It is hard to compare spiritual things with natural things.

We can try to teach the truth and principles of God from the viewpoint of the carnal/natural world, but in reality, this is impossible. Many teachers have attempted to make a living teaching the supernatural from a natural viewpoint. Many have made a lucrative career out of it. However, suppose you test the depth of their knowledge by manifesting the supernatural. In that case, you quickly realize they are all talk and no show. In addition, spiritual teaching is a double-edged sword. The spiritual dimension has a dark side, and we must tread carefully. Hence, we walk in the path of righteousness and not occultism.

The only way to truly teach the supernatural is to teach it from a supernatural realm with the manifestation of God's knowledge, wisdom, and understanding. Carnal teaching puffs up, but spiritual teaching points man to the source of wisdom. The Spirit of God must lead us. His Spirit will lead us and guide us into all truth. A true Spiritual teacher can only teach under the anointing of the Holy Ghost.

The next task we identified was baptism. At first glance, this appears to be strictly a natural task. You take a person. You dunk them into the water. However, we must evaluate why Christian baptism differs from a ritual cleansing baptism at the time of Christ. The answer to this question is found in the word "name" both in Matthew 28:19 and Act 2:38. The Greek word translated as "name" in both these passages is "ónoma." This word has a district connotation to the time of Christ. According to Hebrew notions, a name is inseparable from the person it belongs to. In other words, the "name" is something of his essence. It is the character and reputation of a person. The name is representative of the authority of the person.

Taken from this viewpoint, the act of baptizing someone is not simply an act of getting them wet by dunking them into the water. The act of baptism is a supernatural event performed under the authority of God. The baptism is not for the person performing the action but for the one receiving the baptism.

As the person performing the task of baptizing an individual, we are stepping into a supernatural role. God washes away the sins with the blood of Jesus, buries the old man with Christ, and creates a new creature in Christ Jesus. However, as the ones performing the baptism, we have stepped into a supernatural realm of the authority of Christ. We are the acting representative of God's power and authority to make all things new.

Our next task is to "preach." This task is a great mystery to anyone who has ever preached a message. You can study for hours, prepare the most amazing message, stand before a group of people, deliver it profoundly, and never see a response from the audience. No amount of natural effort can make your preaching effective. Do not get me wrong natural preparation has its merit. However, preaching is in vain if God's supernatural presence and anointing are not in the message.

To the carnal man, preaching is foolishness. The gospel has no impact on a heart that is hardened to receive. Repentance cannot be forced upon a person. A truly repentant heart is only achieved when the Spirit of God moves to draw the heart unto God. No matter how hard you try without the anointing, preaching from a carnal approach will only produce carnal results. To be an effective preacher, you must study to show yourself approved and operate under the anointing of God. There is no room for boasting or self-aggrandizement in true anointed preaching of the gospel.

The preaching of the Word of God is only understood when we see the power of the Word of God in action. We see from the beginning of Genesis how the word of God was able to create. The manifestation of the Word into flesh was able to save, heal, deliver, and make whole.

When we speak the Word of God, it is carried upon the breath that God breathed into man from the beginning. This creative breath can transform the written Word of God into a living manifestation of the Word in action. There is no way carnality can make the preached Word achieve its goal.

Our task of preaching can only be achieved effectively when the Word of God is preached under the anointing power of the Holy Ghost gives life to the Word.

The next task is "observing all the commandments of Christ." Jesus taught many things while he walked upon this earth.

We have the written record of some of His teachings. However, there is much more that was never written.

> *And there are also many other things which Jesus did, the which, if they should be written every one, I suppose that even the world itself could not contain the books that should be written. Amen.*
>
> *John 21:25 (KJV)*

This is why Jesus told His disciples that when the Holy Ghost came, He would teach them all things and lead them into all truth. Our task of observing all the commandments of Christ and teaching others to do the same is not a simple checklist. We can never achieve the level of obedience required simply through carnal effort. We must rely on the leading of the Holy Ghost. How else could we teach all the things Christ commanded without a written record?

I find it extremely interesting that there is unlimited access to the Bible in the day we live. When Peter stood on the day of Pentecost and began to preach, when Paul stood on Mars Hill, or when John the Revelator was boiled in oil, there was no Bible. The Old Testament was a scroll only accessible in synagogues or libraries written in Latin. There was no New Testament. The church of those days did not have Bibles in the back of every pew. Yet today, only some read what we readily have access to. Even fewer observe all the commandments. Let alone seek the Holy Ghost to lead and guild them into all truth.

The next task is "Go into all the world." As with observing all the commandments, the same is true when considering going into all the world. With today's technology, it is easy to travel to the ends of the earth. However, what is our motivation? Going as a tourist is fun, but that is not the task given to the early church. We can quickly sign people up for vacation trips to a remote location. It is easy to get people on a cruise. However, if people are going to leave everything they have and go live in a foreign land, the list is empty.

Going into "all the world" was the location given to perform the task of preaching and every other duty assigned to the early church. We cannot go into "all the world" from our living room. We must get out of our comfort zone and go. Many people are not willing to go. Going to dangerous or uncomfortable locations is not a great motivation in our flesh. It has to be God that directs us where and when to go into the various areas of the world. Going into all the world cannot be done without the supernatural power of the Holy Ghost. Even Paul was restrained by the Holy Ghost from preaching in Asia.

I will group the following three tasks: cast out devils, speak in new tongues, and lay hands on the sick. Without a doubt, we can never perform these tasks on our own. The devils are not subject to us except through the authority of Jesus Christ. Speaking in other tongues is a manifestation of the infilling of the Holy Ghost and a gift of the Spirit. When we lay hands on people, our natural man cannot heal them. These tasks can only be accomplished through the Holy Ghost working in us.

The next task on our list is "losing and retaining the sins of other people." Yet again, losing or retaining another person's sins can only be achieved as a son of God. What authority do we have to forgive sin, except that Christ told us to do it? We know that God is willing to forgive our sins if we ask, and this forgiveness occurs in Heaven. How can we forgive sins? Even to our logical minds, this makes little sense.

From a religious point of view, this almost seems sacrilegious. Nevertheless, it was a commandment of Jesus. I cannot explain how it works and attempt to unpack the theology behind this statement. My only observation is that Jesus commanded His disciples to do it and, by extension, His church.

I know we humans have a terrible habit of holding people's failures over their heads. If we learned to forgive people for their sins against us, it would change the world around us. Many hurts are very deep, and God's Spirit working in us can only achieve true forgiveness. Forgiveness is not simply a set of words we say but an internal change of heart. Repentance is a change in the heart of a sinner, but forgiveness is a change of heart for the victim. We can try to achieve this through our flesh, but we will fail. Only God can help us change our hearts.

We reach the final task we listed from the passages mentioned in this chapter, "Be witnesses." To be a witness, you must have seen something to testify about. A witness is a person who has firsthand knowledge of the events as they transpired. You do not call a person to testify in a court case that did not see what occurred during a crime. Someone who was three states away, told by a friend, who told another friend, who told another person, who finally told the person three states away what happened, would never be called to testify as a witness.

The only way for us to be a witness of Christ is to see firsthand the manifestation of God in our life. How can you testify that God is a healer if you have never seen Him heal? How can you testify that God can change your life if you have never experienced or seen God change your life or someone else's life? We cannot witness what we have not seen. We can read the bible from sunrise to sunset and quote the scripture until we run out of breath, but this does not make us a witness.

The only way we can testify to the power and manifestation of God is to witness the power and manifestation of God firsthand. Once we witness God's hand at work, we can attest to others what we have seen and build their faith. Once their faith is built, God will respond to their faith and manifest the supernatural in their life.

It is time we start witnessing the manifestations of God's power in the world around us. It is time for us to experience the power of God for ourselves and stop reminiscing on the stories of generations past. The experiences of 100, 200, and 2000 years ago are insufficient to replace an authentic personal experience of the power of God in your own life. We cannot relegate the manifestation of God's power to the past. He is a God of the living. He is a God of the now.

We have come full circle. We can agree that God gave Noah a plan. We know that within Noah was the ability to perform the task assigned to him; to build the ark, gather the food, and place the animals on the ark. Now we face a set of tasks that we cannot achieve within ourselves. We require a power beyond us to accomplish the mission laid upon us.

The plan is clear. We must tarry until we are endued by the power from on high. We must receive the infilling of the Holy Ghost. We must be born again of the Spirit. We must become a son of God.

Every task Christ commanded the early church to fulfill was contingent upon this one factor. The earth is waiting for us to step into this role.

> *For the earnest expectation of the creature waiteth for the manifestation of the sons of God.*
>
> *Romans 8:19 (KJV)*

The world is waiting for us. They will only hear the message of salvation if someone preaches it. The only person who can preach it is the one whom God calls. He has called us to be the manifestation of God's glory, image, and presence to those around us. He has commanded us to teach, preach, heal, cast out devils, forgive, and witness to those we encounter every day. We cannot move into the world until we first begin at our Jerusalem. Our Jerusalem is our home and those at our job, school, and community. None of this can be accomplished until we are empowered from on high by the Holy Ghost.

We need to lay aside religion and denominational viewpoints and step into the presence of the living God and seek His face until His power manifests upon us. We become completely immersed in His Spirit and are filled with the Baptism of the Holy Ghost. This is where the plan begins.

The plan is not to build church buildings, ministries, earthly kingdoms, or prestige. The goal is for us to be like Christ, and He will build the church. Not the building but the body of Christ, the church of the living God.

Much more could be said about the plan and its operation. However, no amount of writing can replace a personal experience in the presence of a living God. If we are going to experience rain, it will only happen when we follow the plan.

The Rain is coming

Chapter Six

Therefore thus saith the Lord GOD; I will even rend it with a stormy wind in my fury; and there shall be an overflowing shower in mine anger, and great hailstones in my fury to consume it.
Ezekiel 13:13 (KJV)

We all know that the Word of God is forever settled in Heaven. When God declares something is going to happen. You can be assured it will come to pass. When God spoke to Noah, Noah had no doubt that the Word God said would occur.

And, behold, I, even I, do bring a flood of waters upon the earth, to destroy all flesh, wherein is the breath of life, from under heaven; and every thing that is in the earth shall die. But with thee will I establish my covenant; and thou shalt come into the ark, thou, and thy sons, and thy wife, and thy sons' wives with thee.

Genesis 6:17-18 (KJV)

As we look at this promise to Noah, it is not very uplifting. The Lord simply tells Noah I will destroy the earth with water, but save your family. That is a strong motivating force to build the ark. The unique thing is that God never told Noah how He would bring the flood. He never told Noah how long it would be before the flood came.

All that Noah knew was that water was going to flood the earth. There was no mention of rain. No indication was given to Noah as to when to expect the flood. The only thing given to Noah was a word from the Lord. Noah knew it would happen, and He needed to build the ark.

Many times in the scripture, the Lord sent a word of warning to people, telling them about impending judgments. The Lord works in this way. He will warn people of what is to come. This is not to scare people but to prepare people. If the warning of the judgment had not been given to Noah, he would not have begun preparation.

We can list many prophecies that tell of a time of wrath to come. To go through all of these prophecies would take an entire book. For the moment, we do not need to focus on the judgments to come. Those of us who are familiar with the scripture can quickly point them out.

For those unfamiliar with the scripture, everyone has a sense of dread. Within us is an inner knowledge that we were destined to face judgment and damnation without Christ. No matter what your level of biblical knowledge, a coming judgment is a point of fact that seems to be encoded in us.

For those who desire to know more about prophetic end-time events, many resources and teachers provide various and, at times, contradictory teaching on this subject. For our purposes, we will focus not on the judgment to come but on the deliverance placed within our care.

In the previous chapter, we outlined the plan that God handed down to the church for building a way of escape from the coming judgment. This plan was given to the church to manifest the Kingdom of Heaven, which was to become the ark of safety for the lost to find refuge. The steps to this plan have been laid out in scripture. To focus on the coming judgment without fulfilling God's plan is to step into the role of a slothful servant.

There will come a point in the plan of God where He will tell us the next step to take. As we read in Genesis, we find that point at the beginning of chapter 7.

> *And the LORD said unto Noah, Come thou and all thy house into the ark; for thee have I seen righteous before me in this generation. Of every clean beast thou shalt take to thee by sevens, the male and his female: and of beasts that are not clean by two, the male and his female. Of fowls also of the air by sevens, the male and the female; to keep seed alive upon the face of all the earth. For yet seven days, and I will cause it to rain upon the earth forty days and forty nights; and every living substance that I have made will I destroy from off the face of*

the earth. And Noah did according unto all that the LORD commanded him.

Genesis 7:1-5 (KJV)

When the time came for the rain, God informed Noah. Noah had worked diligently to prepare everything according to God's instructions. Now the rain was on its way. The time had come when all the preparations had been made. The only thing left to do was get in the ark.

Imagine being Noah as he was stepping onto the ark. The world he knew was going to be forever changed. In his lifetime, he watched his great, great, great, great, great, great grandfather Seth die. Then his great, great, great, great, great grandfather Enos died. His great, great, great, great grandfather Cainan died. His great, great, great grandfather Mahalaleel died. His great, great grandfather Jarad died. 12 years ago, his father, Lameck, died. Then the year of the flood, his grandfather Methuselah died. This is fitting given the Hebrew: מְתוּשֶׁלַח, Metušélaḥ, which means "Man of the dart/spear," or alternatively, "his death shall bring judgment."

Now Noah stood on the ramp leading into the Ark to say goodbye to the only world he had ever known. This was the last time he would see all his brothers and sisters or anyone left in his family. Nothing he could have done would have changed their minds. After 75 years of preaching, building, and preparing, his relative did not understand the weight of humanity placed on him from birth.

It is fantastic to study the names and meanings of the patriarchs of the Old Testament. The Hebrew name נֹחַ (Noach) "Noah" means "rest, comfort." There was something about Noah from his birth that even his father, Lameck, saw.

> *And he called his name Noah, saying, This same shall comfort us concerning our work and toil of our hands, because of the ground which the LORD hath cursed.*
>
> *Genesis 5:29 (KJV)*

A generation that desired a savior is the generation into which Noah was born. The people gathered around when his father gave him the name Noah and prophesied over him these words in Genesis 5:29. All these people desired rest from the work of their hands from the ground the Lord had cursed.

Lameck was 56 years old when Adam died. The generation had heard of the Garden of Eden and the provision and splendor of the garden. An angel had been placed east of the Garden of Eden to keep the way. Could this generation still look over into the land occupied by the garden and see its provision but not enter? What a terrible reminder that would have been. Every time they labored to till the ground and plant the seeds, the garden would have served as a visible reminder of the sin of Adam.

Regardless of their ability to see the garden or if they only heard the stories given to them by Adam, the cursing of the ground was always present with them. Even amid the curse, God still brought a harvest to this generation to provide for their need, which they did not see. They saw the curse as more significant than the provision of the provider.

When the son of Lamech was given a plan by God to provide a way to escape, it was not what this generation was looking for. They were looking for the ground to start giving forth its abundance. They desired God to allow them to enter back into the garden. Their view of salvation was returning to the way things were before the fall. But this was not God's plan.

God planned to flood the land. He would use an ark to provide a way of escape from the toil of the ground He has cursed. God planned to destroy the earth as it was and establish an everlasting covenant with mankind.

> *And the bow shall be in the cloud; and I will look upon it, that I may remember the everlasting covenant between God and every living creature of all flesh that is upon the earth. And God said unto Noah, This is the token of the covenant, which I have established between me and all flesh that is upon the earth.*
>
> *Genesis 9:16-17 (KJV)*

Furthermore, the land which had been cursed would be cursed no more.

> *And the LORD smelled a sweet savour; and the LORD said in his heart, I will not again curse the ground any more for man's sake; for the imagination of man's heart is evil from his youth; neither will I again smite any more everything living, as I have done. While the earth remaineth, seedtime and harvest, and cold and heat, and summer and winter, and day and night shall not cease.*
>
> *Genesis 8:21-22 (KJV)*

God reaffirmed the blessing of fruitfulness upon Noah and his sons, and provision was made to provide alternative food sources for all mankind.

> *And God blessed Noah and his sons, and said unto them, Be fruitful, and multiply, and replenish the earth. And the fear of you and the dread of you shall be upon every beast of the earth, and upon every fowl of the air, upon all that moveth upon the earth, and upon all the fishes of the sea; into your hand are they delivered. Every moving thing that liveth shall be meat for you; even as the green herb have I given you all things.*
>
> *Genesis 9:1-3 (KJV)*

The flood that destroyed the earth gave way to a rebirth of blessing upon mankind, a new source of provision, and an everlasting covenant between God and all flesh. The obedience of Noah to the command of God fulfilled the prophecy spoken over him by Lameck. His actions brought comfort to all mankind concerning the work and toil of their hands because of the ground the LORD hath cursed. No longer was man only given food from the cursed land, but the curse on the land was removed, and now man could eat the meat of every moving thing. Now mankind was again blessed by God to be fruitful and multiply and replenish the earth.

What brought destruction to one generation brought blessing and covenant to those that obeyed the word of the Lord. What one generation could not see as a way of salvation became the door to blessing. What brought destruction to a generation of unbelievers became salvation to those who believed.

To the generation of Noah, the flood did not fit within their view of salvation. They could only see the garden as a way of deliverance from the cursed ground. They could recall the stories of Adam about how the Lord had caused the earth to bring forth the herb-yielding seed and the fruit tree yielding fruit. But now, they worked by the sweat of their face to grow herbs, and thistles would grow with them. The Generation of Noah longed for the restoration back to the garden.

If the garden was still visible to them, if they could still see the trees bearing fruit within the garden, what a terrible reminder that would have been. Daily seeing where once man hand access. Now accessing the garden or recreating it was the salvation they longed for. How could destroying the earth with a flood bring salvation? If the garden still existed and mankind could see it, the flood Noah spoke of would destroy the garden.

How rebellious this generation's hearts must have been. The garden was a constant reminder of what God had designed mankind to be. Now man full of the knowledge of good and evil allowed evil to take root. Their imaginations intended to cultivate and protect the garden now were evil continually.

> *And GOD saw that the wickedness of man was great in the earth, and that every imagination of the thoughts of his heart was only evil continually. And it repented the LORD that he had made man on the earth, and it grieved him at his heart.*
>
> *Genesis 6:5-6 (KJV)*

How great the wickedness of their hearts must have been. God could not give them access back into the garden to access the Tree of Life. He had to remove the potential of access and the remainder of the life He had initially intended for man. He had to set His eternal plan of salvation for all humanity in motion. One that Enoch saw a plan which would result in the saving of thousands.

> *And Enoch also, the seventh from Adam, prophesied of these, saying, Behold, the Lord cometh with ten thousands of his saints,*
>
> *Jude 1:14 (KJV)*

The salvation Noah talked about did not fit into the concept of the salvation his generation was looking for. They were looking for the garden, not a flood. Rain was not what they were seeking.

The thing we must understand is the rain was not the flood. The result of the rain was the flood. To those to be saved, the rain became how their salvation became a reality. It was upon the water from the rain that the ark took float. Without the rain, the plan of salvation given to Noah would never have taken place.

At the very moment, Noah was walking onto the Ark, the rain was coming. Did he see the rain clouds? Did he hear the thunder? We do not know. All we know is God told him the rain was coming and to get in the ark.

Noah's obedience to the command culminated in years of labor and anticipation. His family had to be ready. The ark had to be prepared; the food had to be stockpiled.

Today we have a generation that does not understand that rain is coming. They have a desire to see salvation, but is it the salvation spoken of in the scriptures? Are they looking for the restoration of a prior dispensation, or are they looking to the manifestation of God's plan?

> *But this people hath a revolting and a rebellious heart; they are revolted and gone. Neither say they in their heart, Let us now fear the LORD our God, that giveth rain, both the former and the latter, in his season: he reserveth unto us the appointed weeks of the harvest.*
>
> *Jeremiah 5:23-24 (KJV)*

Many today do not see the plan that God has laid out. Looking at the previous chapter, you can see that many of the very things Jesus commissioned the church to do are not even a part of the structure of Christianity today.

Denominations have developed programs, structures, and traditions; the list goes on and on. These all serve a purpose from their point of view. At one time, they seemed the best course of action. My fear and observation are that these elements of modern Christianity have replaced the actual mission and plan God gave to His church. It is not that any of these approaches are incorrect; many are effective to a degree. But when they become the plan by which the church focuses its efforts to direct this world to salvation and neglect the plan God has given His church to birth people into the Kingdom and manifest the Kingdom to the world, we a missing the mark.

Look over the commandments Christ gave the disciples covered in the previous chapter; Wait for the promise of the Holy Ghost, teach, baptize, preach (gospel, repentance, and remission of sins), observe all the commandments of Christ, go into all the world, cast out devils, speak in new tongues, lay hands on the sick, lose or retain sins of another person, and be witnesses. None of these order us to build a big building, establish a lucrative ministry, make a name for ourselves, or start multiple Christian denominations/sects.

The plan is simple; nevertheless, in man's hands, the plan becomes far more complex than Christ's commandments. As Christians, we need to evaluate our efforts in light of the commandments Christ gave.

The rain is coming, but it will only manifest through the plan God has given the church. Miracles, signs, wonders, manifestations of the power of God, healings, Holy Ghost infilling with the evidence of speaking in other tongues are not methods of a bygone generation. These are some of the critical elements established by God to display His glory to the world around us.

If we look back over Christianity, we see the significant moves of God and the revivals of the various centuries past. Building a monument/denomination around a specific person or group is easy. The truth is that all these revivals were trying to guide the church back to God's original plan.

How much different would the church look today if the church had looked back to the entire plan God had given through Christ after each revival? In place of God's view of His church, religious leaders have built on doctrines and concepts developed after the apostles' death to guide their thinking. Many have done away with miracles and healings. The infilling of the Holy Ghost and speaking with other tongues reemerged during the revival of Azusa Street because Christian theologians had rejected the occurrence as satanic.

What is the plan of salvation this modern age of Christianity seeks? From my observations, there is no clear consensus on what the church of God should look like today. It is an "us 4 and no more" group of believers hiding in a church, powerless to change the world around them to some Christian sects. They hide in the church and do not interact with the world because they fear the world will overpower them and make them sin. They have received a get-out-of-hell-free card and do not want to do anything that may cause them to lose their perceived salvation.

To another group, it is prosperity and influence in the world around them. These people see their salvation as a badge of prestige and honor to show off to the world. They give to charity and boast about how blessed they are by God. Some even feel that those less fortunate are somehow not as saved as they are.

There are many other views that I can speak of, but this is not the time to critique. It is the time to instruct. Nothing is wrong with desiring to obtain our eternal reward and remain untainted by the world. There is nothing wrong with being blessed by the Lord and having influence. The problem arises when that becomes your measure of salvation. When the plan you have in mind does not match scripture's plan, we need to change our goal.

God wants you to prosper so you can fulfill His plan. God wants you to be righteous before men so that you will have a good report. But God does not want you to hide in fear of the world nor to flaunt your prosperity over others as if it is by your own power that you have obtained what God has given us.

The rain is coming. We need to be preparing for the church to receive the rain. We are not building a kingdom for ourselves. We are becoming a part of the vehicle God ordained to save this world. The rain is coming.

> *Be glad then, ye children of Zion, and rejoice in the LORD your God: for he hath given you the former rain moderately, and he will cause to come down for you the rain, the former rain, and the latter rain in the first month.*
>
> *Joel 2:23 (KJV)*

It is time for us to prepare for the coming rain. It is time for us to become so consumed with the plan that God has laid out for His church that every aspect of our life resembles His purpose and intent. Each of us has specific skills and talents that God has placed within us. In addition, we have access to Spiritual gifts and calling that are only available through the Holy Ghost. We cannot see our mission without our natural talents, skills, and callings. However, we can never fulfill our purpose without the Spiritual gifts God intended for us to possess.

God is calling sons born into the family of God, the sons of God, to step into the ark of the Kingdom of Heaven and fulfill their purpose. The church does not exist without the sons of God. The Sons of God are powerless outside the role they are meant to accomplish. The sons must be active in the function of the church in fulfilling the commission of Christ. The Kingdom is only accessible to the sons and daughters of God who have been born again.

We can do many things in life when we tap into the innate gifts and callings God has placed within us from birth. Many people have achieved something that seems impossible for others but is obtainable because of their specific gift set. However, many of these achievements were not "God's results." They were just the culmination of carnal actions. God never intended His church to be the result of fleshly efforts. God's church was designed to be the manifestation of His Glory. It is not a "God result" if we can achieve the plan through our own combination of gifts, talents, and callings. God's results only occur through the manifestation of the Spirit of God working through us.

The rain is coming. God has promised in His word that it will happen. He has given a plan to the church with a specific set of tasks for it to perform. What is our next step? How long do we have to prepare? Where are we with regard to the timing of God?

The answer to all these questions can only be found in a relationship with God. Each of us has our own specific role to play. We have our own timeline and set of outcomes for which we are responsible. We do have hope. However, our hope is only found in a relationship with God positioned correctly in His church. It is time to get in the ark. The rain is coming.

> *And it shall come to pass afterward, that I will pour out my spirit upon all flesh; and your sons and your daughters shall prophesy, your old men shall dream dreams, your young men shall see visions: And also upon the servants and upon the handmaids in those days will I pour out my spirit.*
>
> *Joel 2:28-29 (KJV)*

We began this book by looking at the sign of the generation of Noah. We concluded that the sign for our age is the church manifesting the Kingdom of Heaven. This passage of scripture found in Joel gives us insight into the events that unfold as the church enters into its proper role of preparation. When we step into the appropriate plan God ordained for the church, we will see the manifestation of Joel chapter 2 in its fullness.

Many people are looking for the coming of the Lord. They are looking for the world's damnation and the sinners' judgment. Many people just want to be raptured out of this world. They want to be taken to heaven to get out of this "hell on earth," as they call it. There is a problem with that mindset. If the world is displaying the attributes of hell, we, as the church, are failing in our mission. Jesus taught His disciples to pray, "Thy kingdom come thy will be done in earth as it is in Heaven." If the church fulfills its purpose, the earth should not look more like hell. It should look more like heaven.

We will have a wicked testimony when we stand before God and are judged according to the works done in this flesh. When He says, "Why did your generation go to hell? When our response is, "They were so wicked. You should have destroyed them like Sodom and Gomorrah." He will look at us and say, "I gave them you to show them the way to repentance, and you acted like a wicked and slothful servant."

Noah had two prophecies given to his generation. One of judgment and the other of salvation. He could have spent all his time asking the Lord to hurry up. He could have asked God to forgo the plan and get him and his family out of that generation, or he could have preached and built the Ark of Safety. He did the latter.

The rain is coming. Are you working to fulfill God's plan, or are you praying for Him to hurry and get you out and into the garden?

The Preparation

Chapter Seven

The horse is prepared against the day of battle: but safety is of the LORD.
Proverbs 21: 31 (KJV)

We discussed the plan Christ laid out for the church in chapter 5. However, the key to every good project is implementation. Through the death, burial, and resurrection of Jesus Christ, the foundation was laid to initiate God's master plan. God then left the plan's implementation in the hands of the Spirit to lead the church.

The construction of the church is simple. Preach the Word. People hear the preached Word. The Word, once heard, brings faith. God responds to a heart full of faith. God draws upon the faith-filled heart, the heart repents, and the mouth confesses this internal change. The Spirit of Truth brings life, and the process of conception and New Birth has begun.

This process of New Birth was initiated at the inception of the Word into man's heart. This act of insemination of the seed of eternal life. That new life is then birthed through the Water of Baptism and infilling of the Holy Ghost. Where the breath of God fills our spiritual being, the newborn must go on to maturity once this process is initiated.

The plan is simple, yet we complicate it so much. The church has constructed many axillary methods they believe will accomplish the same outcome. However, you must do things God's way to get God's results.

> *But they have not all obeyed the gospel. For Esaias saith, Lord, who hath believed our report? So then faith cometh by hearing, and hearing by the word of God. But I say, Have they not heard? Yes verily, their sound went into all the earth, and their words unto the ends of the world.*
>
> Romans 10:16-18 (KJV)

My question is, "Have you heard what the Lord is speaking to the church?"

We live in a time when the printed Word of God is available to the vast majority of the world, yet many people fail to read the Word. Even fewer hear the Word. We have preachers all over the globe. The Word of God is being preached 24 hours a day, 7 days a week, all over the earth. Yet so few people are listening to what the Lord is speaking. We have libraries full of centuries of religious thought, but who among us is listening for the voice of God?

The preached Word is of great importance to planting the seeds that will help grow the church. However, in many cases, the words presented from the pulpit are based on the words of man's wisdom. There is power in the anointed preached Word. Still, many exchange the power of Truth contained in the Word and witnessed by the Spirit with signs following the traditions and doctrines of man.

Paul knew that it took more than the act of preaching to convert a society. Paul was a very learned man. He sat at the feet of one of the most significant religious minds of his time, Gamaliel. Yet, Paul knew enticing words of man's wisdom would not be adequate to establish the church.

> *And I was with you in weakness, and in fear, and in much trembling. And my speech and my preaching was not with enticing words of man's wisdom, but in demonstration of the Spirit and of power: That your faith should not stand in the wisdom of men, but in the power of God.*
>
> *1 Corinthians 2:3-5 (KJV)*

True Spirit-filled preaching of the Gospel should occur with demonstrations of the Spirit and power. We cannot build a church on our personality or our charisma. We must establish it on the power of God. Our characters may be flawed. Our actions may be imperfect. Our wisdom and understanding may be limited. However, if the church is built on the power and demonstration of the Holy Ghost, if man stumbles and falls, the church will not be shaken. If the pastor dies or moves away, the church does not disband.

The church built on the rock, the foundation upon which Jesus told Peter Jesus would build His church, will not be shaken. The church cannot be destroyed. The gates of hell cannot prevail against a church that is full of the power and demonstration of the Holy Ghost.

As leaders and church members imparticular, we must operate in the full authority of the Spirit of God with the manifestation of the Power and demonstrations. We do not have to rely on the arm of the flesh. We do not have to rely on the teachings of man. We can boldly go before the throne room and speak directly with God. We can inquire of Him, and He will give us wisdom, knowledge, and understanding.

The teachings of man are not to be dismissed. They provide a level of truth. However, everything must be weighed against the truth found in Christ. We must stand not on the teachings of man but on the leading of God.

There is a more sure word of prophecy given to us.

We have also a more sure word of prophecy; whereunto ye do well that ye take heed, as unto a light that shineth in a dark place, until the day dawn, and the day star arise in your hearts: Knowing this first, that no prophecy of the scripture is of any private interpretation. For the prophecy came not in old time by the will of man: but holy men of God spake as they were moved by the Holy Ghost.

2 Peter 1:19-21 (KJV)

I must reiterate that we can hear the Word of God directly from God Himself. We have been given the written Word as a guidepost and standard against which to compare ourselves. If we lack wisdom, we can ask of God. We will fulfill His plan if we hear His voice and harken to His leading in agreement with His written Word.

Are we acting upon what we hear? Are we obeying the voice of the Lord speaking to our lives? Can we truly listen to the voice of God in the hour we are living? Or are we following the traditions and teachings of man? Are we willing to tear apart everything we believe and weigh it against scripture and the leading of the Spirit?

Everything that can be shaken will be shaken. To prepare for the coming rain, we must take apart the ship and ensure we have built it according to God's design. If Noah had built the ark according to his plan, the ark might not have been strong enough to withstand the flood. If he had changed the ark's size, it might not have held the payload it needed to carry.

Prove all things; hold fast that which is good. Abstain from all appearance of evil.

1 Thessalonians 5:21-22 (KJV)

Preparation is not about starting from scratch. It is about ensuring that everything built is according to God's specifications. We cannot take things that God never intended the ark to carry onto the ark. We cannot use building materials God did not command us to use.

We need to learn the voice of God to be adequately prepared. The only way we will be ready is to know His voice.

> *Jesus answered them, I told you, and ye believed not: the works that I do in my Father's name, they bear witness of me. But ye believe not, because ye are not of my sheep, as I said unto you. My sheep hear my voice, and I know them, and they follow me:*
>
> John 10:25-27 (KJV)

These words may seem hard to swallow. But if you do not hear His voice, are you His sheep? If you do not follow His voice, are your deeds demonstrating that He is your Father?

There comes a time in our walk with God when we must stop listening to the voices around us and start listening to the voice of God. There are all kinds of voices trying to speak into our lives daily. The key is distinguishing God's voice from all the other voices speaking to us. Paul explained the nature of multiple voices when he clarified the proper application of the gift of tongues.

> *There are, it may be, so many kinds of voices in the world, and none of them is without signification. Therefore if I know not the meaning of the voice, I shall be unto him that speaketh a barbarian, and he that speaketh shall be a barbarian unto me. Even so ye, forasmuch as ye are zealous of spiritual gifts, seek that ye may excel to the edifying of the church.*
>
> *1 Corinthians 14:10-12 (KJV)*

As we read this, we see a very distinct clue to understanding the voice of God in our lives. The key is found in verse 12, "Seek that you may excel to the edifying of the church." We can listen all day long to the multitude of voices speaking into our lives. Still, the critical outcome is the edification of the church.

If we have not tuned our ears to hear the voice of God, then His voice will sound like a "barbarian" to us. We must know His voice.

This chapter is different from the previous chapters. There is no accurate way to explain to every person the proper steps each of us must take to prepare for what the Lord has called us to do. We are unique, and we all have individual walks with the Lord. The most common component to all of us is that our lives are lived for Christ to bring edification to the church.

There is no harm in education and study, given it is done in pursuit of wisdom, knowledge, understanding, and a constant seeking of the counsel of the Lord. There is no detriment to fasting and giving as long as it is done to build up your faith and not to boast. But above all, we must learn the voice of God.

> *So then faith cometh by hearing, and hearing by the word of God.*
>
> *Romans 10:17 (KJV)*

Faith comes by hearing. You have to be able to hear before your faith can be established. In the discourse of Romans 10, Paul explains that hearing the preached Word gave rise to faith. Once our faith has been established to lead us to enter the Kingdom of Heaven, there is a greater depth of hearing we must experience. We must begin hearing the voice of God for ourselves. We must know His voice. How will we know when to prepare for action if we do not know His voice? How will we be ready to step into our calling if we do not know His voice?

We can learn all the elements laid out in the scriptures to accomplish the plan. We can know every word spoken by Christ recorded in the Gospels, but if we cannot hear His voice, we are useless in the time of battle. How will we be prepared to run into the fight to rescue the fallen? How will we be ready to speak life to those around us? We must hear God's voice.

Our mission is to manifest the Gospel in power and demonstration. Every moment God has given us is an opportunity to display His glory and power to the world. It is not our job to build the church. Our job is to be the church and manifest the Kingdom of Heaven.

> *And I say also unto thee, That thou art Peter, and upon this rock I will build my church; and the gates of hell shall not prevail against it.*
>
> *Matthew 16:18 (KJV)*

The great thing about the age we live in is that we do not have to build a church. Christ said He would build the church. That takes this task out of our hands and places it into the supernatural hands of God Himself. Our job is to listen and obey His voice so we can do our part to facilitate the manifestation of His Kingdom.

As we have said, the church is made up of each individual son of God tightly fit together to achieve God's purpose. We have been given the gospel of the Kingdom. We have been given the power to demonstrate the supernatural. We have been given the privilege to be a part of the church, the manifestation of the body of Christ to the world today. Our task is to declare the message and manifest the kingdom of Heaven.

So how do we prepare?

Once the ark was built, the preparation was complete. The Lord then gave the orders to Noah to go into the Ark. Noah had to know the voice of God for this entire process to take place. How would the Ark have been built if Noah did not hear the voice of God? How would Noah have known when to enter the Ark if he did not listen to the voice of God?

> *And the LORD said unto Noah, Come thou and all thy house into the ark; for thee have I seen righteous before me in this generation.*
>
> *Genesis 7:1 (KJV)*

Although the Ark was prepared, Noah was not aware of the timing of the judgment to come. There was no clue when God was going to send the rain. All Noah could do was build the ark, gather provisions, and prepare to bring the animals onto the ark. Until Noah received a fresh Word from the Lord, all Noah could do was wait.

Then the Word came.

> *And they that went in, went in male and female of all flesh, as God had commanded him: and the LORD shut him in.*
>
> *Genesis 7:16 (KJV)*

The first step in the process is doing what you can do. We see a great lesson as we look over the events leading up to Noah entering the Ark. Noah did what Noah could do. This is the first step in everything God calls us to accomplish. We must start by doing what we can do. We must prepare, but we can only do what we are capable of doing, and God must do the rest.

There are things that we cannot do in our own strength. We must realize that a time will come when God steps on the scene and does what only He can do. We must understand that our efforts do not bring about these God moments in our lives. Many people fail to realize that when God shows up, it is all about Him. No matter what we have done leading up to that moment, our efforts are trivial to God's miraculous manifestation.

Often God will instruct us to do something not because it plays so perfectly into His plan but to try our obedience. Think about the animals that Noah brought into the ark. God could have spoken and made all those animals again just at His Word if God desired. Noah played a role in preserving the animals, but God created them all. Noah's task was to look after something God could fix if Noah didn't get it right.

So does that mean we stop trying, or do we need to not focus on the things God is capable of doing Himself? God forbid. We need to do whatever God asks of us. We need to be prepared for anything.

The horse is prepared against the day of battle: but safety victory is of the LORD.

Proverbs 21: 31 (KJV)

Let us look at it this way. God is trying to train us as children. When we raise a child, we know they will have to learn a specific skill to achieve success in life. We do not start them off focused on the task they will have to accomplish when they are older. We start them off with simple tasks.

For instance, as adults, we must maintain a balanced budget based on our income and expenses. In some cases, this can be a very complex task to achieve. The more bills you have to pay, the harder it becomes to properly manage the calculations and ensure you do not overdraft your account. You could get in major trouble if you spend more than you make.

We must teach our kids this life skill so that they will achieve this task when they get older. Do we hand them the family checkbook and say handle its finances? Not a chance.

The first thing we must do is teach them to count. Then we teach them math. Next, we teach them the value of money. We start them on an allowance and move up to more complex money management life skills. Nevertheless, each of these steps prepares for the final task in their adult life.

God prepares us in much the same way. We may not understand the training process or the steps we are taking. They may not even be logically connected to what we feel our calling is. Nevertheless, each lesson prepares us and leads us closer to fulfilling our ultimate purpose in God's plan.

> *Of these things put them in remembrance, charging them before the Lord that they strive not about words to no profit, but to the subverting of the hearers. Study to shew thyself approved unto God, a workman that needeth not to be ashamed, rightly dividing the word of truth. But shun profane and vain babblings: for they will increase unto more ungodliness. And their word will eat as doth a canker: of whom is Hymenaeus and Philetus;*
>
> *2 Timothy 2:14 (KJV)*

Our preparation must begin with studying. We must take it upon ourselves to learn the Word of God. We must hide it in our hearts. We must remember His Word. David, in Psalm 119, expounds upon this concept.

> *Wherewithal shall a young man cleanse his way? By taking heed thereto according to thy word. With my whole heart have I sought thee: O let me not wander from thy commandments. Thy word have I hid in mine heart, that I might not sin against thee. Blessed art thou, O LORD: teach me thy statutes. With my lips have I declared all the judgments of thy mouth. I have rejoiced in the way of thy testimonies, as much as in all riches. I will meditate in thy precepts, and have respect unto thy ways. I will delight myself in thy statutes: I will not forget thy word.*
>
> *Psalm 119:9-16 (KJV)*

We must prepare by taking heed to His Word, seeking Him with our whole hearts, not wandering from His commandments, hiding His Word in our hearts, and meditating on His precepts so we do not forget them.

The Hebrew word for meditate שִׂיחַ (siach), which means to muse, complain, or talk of. The root of this word indicates an action of speaking to oneself aloud. We have talked about the breath of God previously and the power of the spoken word. There is great power in setting and speaking the Word of God to yourself aloud. The Word of God becomes empowered by the creative breath God placed in you. Your ears hear the Word spoken, and your faith is built up. As we mentioned earlier, faith cometh by hearing and hearing by the Word of God.

The Word of God is replete with commandments and tasks that can be implemented into your life and daily regimens. However, creating a list of hurdles you must jump through is not preparation. The Key to truly studying the Word of God is hearing God speak through His Word to you.

Old Testament Israel made this mistake. They treated the law of sacrifices and New Moons as a way to appease God to get from God what they wanted. God became sick of this approach and desired Israel to change their hearts.

To what purpose is the multitude of your sacrifices unto me? saith the LORD: I am full of the burnt offerings of rams, and the fat of fed beasts; and I delight not in the blood of bullocks, or of lambs, or of he goats.

When ye come to appear before me, who hath required this at your hand, to tread my courts? Bring no more vain oblations; incense is an abomination unto me; the new moons and sabbaths, the calling of assemblies, I cannot away with; it is iniquity, even the solemn meeting. Your new moons and your appointed feasts my soul hateth: they are a trouble unto me; I am weary to bear them. And when ye spread forth your hands, I will hide mine eyes from you: yea, when ye make many prayers, I will not hear: your hands are full of blood.

Wash you, make you clean; put away the evil of your doings from before mine eyes; cease to do evil; Learn to do well; seek judgment, relieve the oppressed, judge the fatherless, plead for the widow.

Come now, and let us reason together, saith the LORD: though your sins be as scarlet, they shall be as white as snow; though they be red like crimson, they shall be as wool. If ye be willing and obedient, ye shall eat the good of the land: But if ye refuse and rebel, ye shall be devoured with the sword: for the mouth of the LORD hath spoken it.

Isaiah 1:11-20 (KJV)

Our preparation should not be based on rigorous rules and regulations or religiously performing activities. Our preparation should be based on our relationship with God and hearing His voice.

We must get into the true church and stir up the gifts of God that have been placed within us. However, nothing can replace hearing God's voice for ourselves. The most critical step to preparing is learning to hear God's voice.

On a final note in this chapter on preparations, let us look at Paul's closing statement in a portion of the scripture we mentioned earlier.

> *See that none render evil for evil unto any man; but ever follow that which is good, both among yourselves, and to all men. Rejoice evermore. Pray without ceasing. In every thing give thanks: for this is the will of God in Christ Jesus concerning you. Quench not the Spirit. Despise not prophesyings. Prove all things; hold fast that which is good. Abstain from all appearance of evil.*
>
> *1 Thessalonian 5:15-22 (KJV)*

The task of preparation is upon us all. We must be instant in season and out of season. We must be ready when God speaks to us to move so that we will be prepared for what God calls us to do. Each moment of our existence is an opportunity for God to display His glory. God uses people to achieve this goal. We must be ready, willing, and able to step forth when He speaks.

In his closing remarks in 1 Thessalonians, we see that Paul is attempting to give a set of guidelines for the church in Thessalonica to follow to help keep them on course to fulfilling their mission. In this passage, Paul mentions rejoicing, praying, giving thanks, and several other actions to this set of early believers. Our preparation cannot be without these activities.

No matter how prepared we feel or what level of success we have achieved, we must realize that it is not for our exaltation. Nothing we achieve as born-again sons of God is for our glory.

God invites us to join Him in manifesting His vision and purpose in the world He created. He can achieve His goal without us. However, He has provided an opportunity for us to be active participants.

A person who is truly prepared to see the revival rain that is to come is one who is willing to do anything the Lord asks without hesitation. We must be willing to sacrifice ourselves to manifest God's glory.

When Noah stepped into the Ark, and the door closed behind him, there was no turning back or alternative. Noah was locked into an ark totally dependent on God's supernatural plan.

God is waiting for us to take that step and lock ourselves in with Him. Let Him close every door that does not lead to His purpose and trust in His supernatural plan. The rain is coming.

Entering the Ark

Chapter Eight

For as in the days that were before the flood they were eating and drinking, marrying and giving in marriage, until the day that Noe entered into the ark,
Matthew 24: 38 (KJV)

For the Ark to be an effective point of rescue, Noah and his family had to enter. Knowing that the manifestation of the Kingdom of Heaven by the church is the mechanism God selected to rescue fallen man is of little use if we fail to enter.

Verily, verily, I say unto you, He that entereth not by the door into the sheepfold, but climbeth up some other way, the same is a thief and a robber.
John 10: 1 (KJV)

It is one thing to know of a door to freedom. It is yet another thing to look for a way around that door. But this concept of entering we are talking about holds a far greater level of significance than just how we enter the Kingdom.

Many people are looking for a way into eternity on their terms. The religious culture of the Christian church over the millennia has attempted to create its own unique doorways into the Kingdom based on denominational views or personal convictions.

As the lost world watches the church, we struggle with the location of the Door. The provision is beyond the door. The safety is beyond the door. The plan is only fulfilled beyond the door. The future generations only find their inheritance beyond the door.

All the planning and all the work are of no value if you don't enter the door. The rain will not come until we have entered through the door.

I am the door: by me if any man enter in, he shall be saved, and shall go in and out, and find pasture.

John 10: 9 (KJV)

Jesus is the Door. He is the way; there is no other path into the Kingdom. We have talked about becoming a son of God and the protection of sons. However, we must understand that the sonship offered through Christ is much more.

A birthing process is designed to give us entrance into the Kingdom of Heaven. Jesus held a conversation with Nicodemus that provided great clarity as to the process of entering the Kingdom.

There was a man of the Pharisees, named Nicodemus, a ruler of the Jews: The same came to Jesus by night, and said unto him, Rabbi, we know that thou art a teacher come from God: for no man can do these miracles that thou doest, except God be with him. Jesus answered and said unto him, Verily, verily, I say unto thee, Except a man be born again, he cannot see the kingdom of God. Nicodemus saith unto him, How can a man be born when he is old? can he enter the second time into his mother's womb, and be born? Jesus answered, Verily, verily, I say unto thee, Except a man be born of water and of the Spirit, he cannot enter into the kingdom of God. That which is born of the flesh is flesh; and that which is born of the Spirit is spirit. Marvel not that I said unto thee, Ye must be born again. I am the door: by me if any man enter in, he shall be saved, and shall go in and out, and find pasture.

John 3: 1-7 (KJV)

In Jesus' discourse with Nicodemus, we see a very striking statement. Jesus makes two distinctive regarding the Kingdom. One is the ability to see the Kingdom, and the other is the ability to enter the Kingdom.

If we truly desire to enter ther Kingdom, we need to know the proper way to the entrance. Jesus specifically indicated that the process of being born of the water and the spirit are the keys that grant you access to enter the Kingdom.

This simple statement put to rest all the other arguments posed by the various sects of the Christian religion. A sinner's prayer will not grant you entrance to the Kingdom. Shaking a preacher's hand will not open the door to the Kingdom. Water baptism alone will not unlock the door. Signing a membership card or holding an ordination with a denomination does not open the door to the Kingdom.

He is the way, the truth, the light, and the Door. If He defined the requirements for entry as being born of the water and the Spirit, He would not accept a substitute.

Many may be asking why I have taken such a hard stand concerning how we enter the Kingdom. The truth of the matter is that I am only taking the Biblical stance laid out by Jesus. The reason for this clarification is the importance of entering the door.

When we read the passage in Matthew 24: 38 and Luke 17: 27, we see a very telling observation about Noah entering the Ark.

> *For as in the days that were before the flood they were eating and drinking, marrying and giving in marriage, until the day that Noe entered into the ark,*
>
> *Matthew 24: 38 (KJV)*

> *They did eat, they drank, they married wives, they were given in marriage, until the day that Noe entered into the ark, and the flood came, and destroyed them all.*
>
> *Luke 17: 27 (KJV)*

In both of these accounts, the people of Noah's time were going about their daily lives unto Noah entered the Ark. We have made the distinction throughout this book of the importance of the manifestation of the Kingdom of Heaven. We must understand that the world is watching us. The world reads our lives daily, looking for evidence that what we say aligns with how we live and act.

Ye are our epistle written in our hearts, known and read of all men:

2 Corinthians 3:2 (KJV)

The world is longing to see authenticity. So many things act the part but are not real. So many people wear masks and inwardly are the opposite of what they portray. They are looking for the sign. They are waiting to see if the hope we preach, the peace we have, the joy we possess, the love we share, and the faith we hold to are real.

When the generation alive during Noah's time faced the message of impending destruction, they had two options. Option one, wait and see what happens, and option two, respond to the message.

For the generation of Noah, their response was to wait. How many people in our generation are waiting to see if what the church is preaching will come to pass?

The problem we are faced with is that the response of the people is predicated upon their observation. Access to the Bible provides a clear avenue for people to read what the manifestation of the Kingdom of Heaven and the church should look like. As a point of fact, the Bible even gives us a well-documented example of the culture and actions of the early church.

Our problem is that the church at large does not resemble this example. Many Christian denominations have relegated the miracles, the gifts of the Spirit, and even the culture of the early church to a bygone day that was only applicable during the time it was written.

This line of logic, if followed through, leaves us with a Bible that becomes irrelevant to the modern age we are living in. But what if the example and events of the early church were simply launching points for us? The Kingdom of Heaven is one of the main topics addressed during the ministry of Jesus. In fact, the only Gospel He preached was the gospel of the Kingdom.

I strongly believe that the Kingdom of Heaven should be more visible today than it was during the lives of the early church. However, this is not the case. The world is looking for it. The world desires the children of the Kingdom to mature and step into their rightful position.

> *For I reckon that the sufferings of this present time are not worthy to be compared with the glory which shall be revealed*

in us. For the earnest expectation of the creature waiteth for the manifestation of the sons of God. For the creature was made subject to vanity, not willingly, but by reason of him who hath subjected the same in hope, Because the creature itself also shall be delivered from the bondage of corruption into the glorious liberty of the children of God. For we know that the whole creation groaneth and travaileth in pain together until now. And not only they, but ourselves also, which have the firstfruits of the Spirit, even we ourselves groan within ourselves, waiting for the adoption, to wit, the redemption of our body.

Romans 8: 18-23 (KJV)

We see in this passage that creation itself is in bondage. Everything that God created is groaning, waiting with anticipation for something to take place.

Two events become apparent from this passage. The first is the manifestation of the sons of God. The second is the appearance of the glorious liberty of the children of God.

Many people have never thought about what the indications of these two events have in common or what these two events even are. To better understand these events, we must look into the Greek.

The Greek word "huios" is used in this passage and is translated as "sons." This differs from the Greek word "teknon, " translated as "children" in this passage. There is some indication that the word "huios/sons" is a child that has reached the age of maturity. A son that is old enough to step into the position of a leader in his household. A son who is old enough to inherit his authority. On the other hand, the "teknon/children" refers to a descendant who still possesses child-like characteristics. This word is also translated as "son" (examples Matthew 21:28, Mark 2:5).

The two events outlined in this passage show us that creation itself has been subjected to the bondage of corruption or decay. That creation is groaneth and travailing in pain. But why? I could do a very deep word study and expound on this concept, but I will keep it simple. When Adam lost his dominion over creation, creation was placed in bondage and decay, to the point that when Satan tempted Jesus, Satan was in possession of the dominion Adam once held. Creation wants us to grow up.

Why is the distinction between immature sons and mature sons important? Because it gives us an understanding of what is required to operate under the authority of the Kingdom.

> *Now I say, That the heir, as long as he is a child, differeth nothing from a servant, though he be lord of all; But is under tutors and governors until the time appointed of the father. Even so we, when we were children, were in bondage under the elements of the world: But when the fulness of the time was come, God sent forth his Son, made of a woman, made under*

the law, To redeem them that were under the law, that we might receive the adoption of sons. And because ye are sons, God hath sent forth the Spirit of his Son into your hearts, crying, Abba, Father. Wherefore thou art no more a servant, but a son; and if a son, then an heir of God through Christ.

Galatians 4: 1-7 (KJV)

This passage provides great insight into the requirement of maturity as a prerequisite for authority. It is only fitting to denote that the Greek word used for "child" in verse one is "teknon." And the Greek word used for "sons" in verse six is "huios."

We must understand that Christ commissioned those gathered on a mount in Galilee. He charged them to go and make disciples. A disciple in Greek is "one who studies or is a student." Let's look at the purpose of the fivefold ministry in the context of making disciples. We see that the end goal of the fivefold ministry is to bring us all into the full stature of Christ. Or, in simple terms, for us to grow up and be a mature example of Christ.

You may wonder why I have taken you to this point when this chapter is about entering the Ark. We must understand that Christ came to establish a Kingdom. The governing body of this Kingdom is the church. The Greek word "ekklesia" is translated as "church." Jesus did not create this word; it was a term used in the political realm of the time. It originated from the Greeks and was carried into the Roman Empire.

The Ekklesia was a group of people much like the United States Senate. However, this ekklesia was commissioned with the task of taking the edicts of the Ceasar and making them into law, and enacting and enforcing the heart of the empire. The Ekklesia had power within both the Greek and Roman empires. They were responsible for setting the legal criterion for citizenship and the benefits associated with this status.

Within the Kingdom of Heaven, the church holds great authority. However, this authority can not be obtained or exercised if those occupying the church's seats are not mature. Suppose they are still little children and have not spiritually developed into the full stature of Christ. In that case, they are no different than a servant.

All of creation is waiting for the sons of God to grow up. The dominion Adam once ruled, the kingdom Jesus came to establish His rule over, is waiting for the glorious liberty that is the possession of the children of God to manifest.

This redemption offered through Jesus Christ is bigger than us. It is bigger than humanity. Creation is waiting for us to enter the Kingdom and exercise the authority of mature sons of God.

> *For God so loved the world, that he gave his only begotten Son, that whosoever believeth in him should not perish, but have everlasting life. For God sent not his Son into the world to condemn the world; but that the world through him might be saved.*

John 3: 16-17 (KJV)

Many people can quote this passage of scripture, and it holds great significance in my heart as well as many others. One day I was studying this passage. I was astonished to learn that the Greek word used for "world" in this passage is "kosmos." Most people understand the English word cosmos. The meaning is not humanity. It refers to the expanse of the universe. Oddly, John used this Greek word in reference to the object of God's love.

If we compare the Greek word "kosmos" to the Greek word "gé," which means "earth," we see that there is something deeper than the religious connotation of cosmos referring to only mankind.

> *He that cometh from above is above all: he that is of the earth is earthly, and speaketh of the earth: he that cometh from heaven is above all.*
>
> *John 3:31 (KJV)*

John uses the word "ge" in this passage just 15 verses after he uses the word "kosmos." Christ came to be the savior of the cosmos, not just humanity. There is a greater weight to the sacrifice of Christ than just the redemption of mankind. The redemption of the whole of creation rested upon it.

And we have seen and do testify that the Father sent the Son to be the Saviour of the world.

1 John 4:14 (KJV)

There is a great task placed upon us. The Kingdom of God is coming, and we are the portals through which the Glory of God is expressed. Jesus instructed His disciples to pray that the Kingdom would come. We have been given the keys to this Kingdom and have the opportunity to exercise dominion until Christ returns.

To wit, that God was in Christ, reconciling the world unto himself, not imputing their trespasses unto them; and hath committed unto us the word of reconciliation.

2 Corinthians 5:19 (KJV)

The people of this earth are watching and listening to our message. They go about their daily tasks but are aware of the church. The problem is that the people who call themselves Christians have never entered the Kingdom.

The generation of Noah was watching the building of the Ark. They watched as the provision was collected and the animals gathered. They knew what Noah was preaching. But it did not become a reality to them until Noah entered the Ark.

Many people read over the fact that God instructed Noah to enter the Ark 7 days before the rain began and the fountains of the deep opened up. The flood did not force Noah into the ark. Noah's obedience to the word of God was the motivating force that led Noah to enter the Ark.

We have many people looking at the events in the world. People are watching the signs of the times. They are taking note of the wars and rumors of wars. The earthquakes, severe weather, famine, drought, and the myriad of other things going on are the focus of not only the people of the world but also the members of most churches.

Creation is groaning not because the Lord is coming but because it is waiting for the sons of God to step into their authority. If the people of the earth would turn their eyes towards the Glory of God, if the church would grow up and begin to take on the authority of a Son of God, if we would truly enter the Kingdom and not just sit back and talk about it, this world would take notice.

Our problem is if we wait too long, the door will be shut, and we may not be inside. The cosmos is waiting for us, the people of this earth are waiting for us, and God is waiting for us. Why are we not stepping into the Kingdom?

The rain cannot begin until we enter the Kingdom. People are waiting for God to give us more power, more authority, and more of whatever we think we lack. The truth is we have been given everything pertaining to righteousness. We have been given all power in heaven and earth contained within His name. Yet we fail to operate in what we have been given. Why would He give us more when we do not even operate in what we have been given?

The Outpouring

Chapter Nine

I indeed have baptized you with water: but he shall baptize you with the Holy Ghost.
Mark 1:8 (KJV)

We have found grace in the eyes of the Lord. We have learned to hear the voice of God. We have been born into the family of God and are now His sons. We have the plan and are implementing the plan given to us by Jesus Himself. We have prepared. We know the rain is coming. Now is the time of the great outpouring.

> *And it came to pass after seven days, that the waters of the flood were upon the earth. In the six hundredth year of Noah's life, in the second month, the seventeenth day of the month, the same day were all the fountains of the great deep broken up, and the windows of heaven were opened. And the rain was upon the earth forty days and forty nights.*
> Genesis 7:10-12 (KJV)

Many people have read this scripture passage and assumed that the flood of Noah's time was simply a matter of a great outpouring of rain. However, if we look a little closer at the passage, we see two events that led to the waters of the flood being upon the earth. The first event that occurred was the breaking up of all the fountains of the deep.

Many have hypothesized about what their fountains may have been. The Hebrew word means "spring," like a water spring. No matter what this event may have looked like, the amount of water in these fountains combined with the rain was sufficient to cause the flood over the entire earth.

It is interesting to note that the breaking open of the fountains of the deep is mentioned prior to the windows of heaven being opened.

How does this equate to our current dispensation? What analogy could be drawn between the fountains of the deep and the outpouring of the latter rain?

Let us first look at the first occurrence of the church being filled with the Holy Ghost. Many have equated the former rain to the first time the Holy Ghost poured out upon man.

As we examine this event, we will look for an analogy of the fountains of the deep.

> *And when the day of Pentecost was fully come, they were all with one accord in one place. And suddenly there came a sound*

> *from heaven as of a rushing mighty wind, and it filled all the house where they were sitting. And there appeared unto them cloven tongues like as of fire, and it sat upon each of them. And they were all filled with the Holy Ghost, and began to speak with other tongues, as the Spirit gave them utterance.*
>
> *Acts 2: 1-4 (KJV)*

What an amazing event this must have been. The early believers followed the plan laid out for them by Jesus to wait in Jerusalem. Then the Holy Ghost manifested in their midst.

Was this event truly the first outpouring of the "rain" of the Holy Ghost? Nowhere in this passage does it mention rain or outpouring. Maybe there is a further hint in Peter's message in this chapter. As we begin to read Peter's message, he quotes a passage from Joel 2:28.

> *And it shall come to pass in the last days, saith God, I will pour out of my Spirit upon all flesh: and your sons and your daughters shall prophesy, and your young men shall see visions, and your old men shall dream dreams:*
>
> *Acts 2:17 (KJV)*

This passage does definitively indicate that Peter equated the events that occurred in the Upper Room on the day of Pentecost with the pouring out of the Spirit of God spoken of by Joel. He even further indicates that this promise mentioned in Joel is a result of the death, burial, and resurrection of Jesus Christ and His assertion into heaven later in this message.

> *Therefore being by the right hand of God exalted, and having received of the Father the promise of the Holy Ghost, he hath shed forth this, which ye now see and hear.*
>
> *Acts 2: 33 (KJV)*

In the passage above, Peter specifically indicates that the events seen and heard by those in Jerusalem resulted from the Holy Ghost being "shed forth." The Greek word translated as "shed" is ἐκχέω (ekcheo) which means "pour." This is the same Greek word used for "pour out," as Peter quoted Joel in verse 17.

We can logically conclude that this was the outpouring of the Holy Ghost. In the context of something being poured out from heaven, it would not be hard to correlate this with a rain of the Spirit. However, there is no mention or inference of fountains of the deep.

Where are the fountains of the deep? To get a better handle on this question, let us look at one of the times Jesus mentioned the Holy Ghost coming to dwell within man.

> *And I will pray the Father, and he shall give you another Comforter, that he may abide with you forever;*

> *Even the Spirit of truth; whom the world cannot receive, because it seeth him not, neither knoweth him: but ye know him; for he dwelleth with you, and shall be in you.*
>
> John 14: 16-17 (KJV)

Jesus indicates that the Holy Ghost will be dwelling within the believers. This Comforter would also abide with the believers forever. Yet still, no indication is given of a fountain of the deep.

Another passage of scripture may shed some light on the fountains. The writer of the gospel of John references the Holy Ghost and a flow of water.

> *He that believeth on me, as the scripture hath said, out of his belly shall flow rivers of living water.*
> *But this spake he of the Spirit, which they that believe on him should receive: for the Holy Ghost was not yet given; because that Jesus was not yet glorified.*
>
> John 7: 38-39 (KJV)

What an amazing analogy is given by Jesus in this statement. Jesus distinctly indicates that the believer will have a river of living water flowing out of them. Something deep within a believer would contain a constant flow. Then the writer of John specifies that the source of this river was the indwelling of the Holy Ghost.

Within every Holy Ghost, filled son of God, is a river, a fountain that is designed to flow. We should not stop the flow of the Spirit from within us. The infilling of the Holy Ghost was designed to establish the outward flow of the Spirit into the world around us. Much like the fountains of the deep mentioned in Genesis, there is a fountain deep within each son of God.

What is the importance of understanding this analogy? As we mentioned early, the fountains of the deep breaking up preceded the rain. We are the fountains that must be broken up and begin to flow forth.

The outpouring occurs when we pour ourselves out into the lives of the empty vessels around us, just as the widow gathered all the empty vessels into her home and poured out the oil until all were filled.

The Lord has placed His oil within us, and as we pour out the anointing, His presence will manifest to refill us to keep our vessels full and overflowing.

The church was never designed to be the storehouse of the Spirit of God. We are the temples of the Holy Ghost. His Spirit resides within us. As we walk through our day, we carry His Spirit. This life-giving Spirit was not given to us to contain and control. It was given to us so it would flow from us like a river.

To allow the Spirit to flow, we must relinquish control. The Spirit of God is the power of creation itself. When we try to control the flow of the Spirit in our lives, we hinder the creation of the future God intended for us.

The greatest problem with the Christian religion today is that people have forsaken the flow of the fountain of living water. They have replaced the manifestation and flow of the Spirit of God with tradition, catechisms, creeds, and denominational stances. The river of living water can never be replaced with a cistern of religion.

> *For My people have committed two evils: They have forsaken Me, The fountain of living waters, To hew for themselves cisterns, Broken cisterns That can hold no water.*
>
> *Jeremiah 2:13 (KJV)*

This is a hard statement. Have we, as the church, become the Nation of Israel during the time of Jeremiah? Do we have the flow of the fountain of living waters flowing through our life, our day, and our appointed times of worship, or have we created cisterns that hold no manifestation of the flow of the Spirit?

We cannot afford church as usual if we desire to see the outpouring. We should never be able to conduct a worship service and preach a message and never feel or see a manifestation of the presence of God. Suppose all we have is a designated time that we gather together to meet as a group, and God does not need to be present for the event to be a success. Are we truly following the plan?

It is time we rethink our efforts. There has got to be a special manifestation of God upon each of us that is tangible and felt by others in our life. There must be a flow of the Spirit of God living inside of us that cannot be contained.

The Holy Spirit flowing out of us like rivers of living water will result in the opening of the blinded eyes, the healing of the sick, the raising of the dead, the gifts of the Spirit, and so much more. Our lives should be supernatural encounters every moment of our day. The question is, why are we not seeing these in our lives today?

If you take a cup and pour coffee into the cup and bring it about to the rim, is it completely full? You can be almost full but still have a little room for more. If you set that cup on a table and never move it, the coffee will never overflow or pour out of the cup. To the person looking at the outside of the cup, there is no difference between that cup and one that is empty. Now if you pour coffee into the cup until it runs over the rim, the cup is full and overflowing.

Suppose we remain in a state where we experience God but do not allow His spirit to overflow from our inward being. In that case, the world will never experience the power God has placed within us. Man cannot look into the soul of someone to determine the level of the Spirit of God they operate in. The only way the world can see God is by allowing His Spirit to Flow out of your inward being into the world around you.

God does not want us to be partially filled; He wants us to overflow with the power of the Holy Ghost. We cannot become stagnant pools of living water. Suppose you have ever walked upon a pool of water that has remained in a trench for any length of time without freshwater entering and flowing through it. In that case, the water is stagnant and smells of death.

God does not want us to become stagnant. He wants us to leak out onto the world around us. Everywhere we go, we should leave a puddle of God's Spirit. If we never allow the Spirit to flow through us or we do not get a refreshing refill of the Holy Ghost that manifests in a flow of living water out of us, we will become stagnant. No wonder after some Christians leave the room, you can still smell the putrid aroma of their presence. Instead of leaving the fragrance of heaven, they carry around the stagnant dying remains of the plan God has for their life.

God did not give us His spirit to live on the touch we received 20 years ago. He gave us His Spirit so we can commune with Him daily and receive a fresh outpouring of His Spirit into our souls daily. God desires our souls to prosper. He desires to pour into us all the wisdom, knowledge, and understanding He has. However, this can only happen through an intimate daily relationship.

Now the God of hope fill you with all joy and peace in believing, that ye may abound in hope, through the power of the Holy Ghost.

Romans 15:13 (KJV)

What an amazing statement from Paul. We can abound in hope through the power of the Holy Ghost. The Greek word translated here as "abound" is περισσεύω (perisseuó) which means to exceed, go beyond the expected measure, to overflow. God desires us to overflow in hope through the power of the Holy Ghost.

When we enact the plan God has given the church, we must allow the Spirit to flow through us to manifest the supernatural. By allowing the living river to flow through us, we will abound in hope and the power of the Holy Ghost.

So many people are waiting for power to be endued upon us. If we have received the infilling of the Holy Ghost, it resides within us. We have received an anointing of power.

But the anointing which ye have received of him abideth in you, and ye need not that any man teach you: but as the same anointing teacheth you of all things, and is truth, and is no lie, and even as it hath taught you, ye shall abide in him.

1 John 2:27 (KJV)

The Greek word used here for anointing is χρίσμα (xrísma), meaning anointing or unction. It refers to the teaching ministry of the Holy Spirit, guiding the receptive believer into the fullness of God's preferred will. The Holy Ghost will lead us and guide us. A force/power within the Holy Ghost-filled son of God will flow out of us if we allow it to.

Jesus was anointed to perform the ministry to which He was called. We all have our unique ministry and calling. The Spirit lives within us to help us achieve our purpose. We need to let the flow of the anointing guide our path.

> *The Spirit of the Lord is upon me, because he hath anointed me to preach the gospel to the poor; he hath sent me to heal the brokenhearted, to preach deliverance to the captives, and recovering of sight to the blind, to set at liberty them that are bruised, To preach the acceptable year of the Lord. 20 And he closed the book, and he gave it again to the minister, and sat down. And the eyes of all them that were in the synagogue were fastened on him. And he began to say unto them, this day is this scripture fulfilled in your ears.*
>
> *Luke 4: 18-21 (KJV)*

The anointing of Jesus is without debate. The scriptures prophesied about His anointing. The gospels tell the stories of the manifestation of this anointing. This anointing affected His teaching, His deliverance, and his healing ministry. It was the anointing that made the difference.

> *And it shall come to pass in that day, that his burden shall be taken away from off thy shoulder, and his yoke from off thy neck, and the yoke shall be destroyed because of the anointing.*
> Isaiah 10:27 (KJV)

It is the anointing that breaks the yoke. Many in the religious world are yoked to traditions, teachings, doctrines of men, and denominational lines. These yokes prevent the flow of the Spirit. When the Lord speaks to us to do something, and we begin to think through our belief system to determine if we should obey or not, that belief system is a yoke.

Many fear they have no anointing because they are not the pastor or the evangelist. This is a yoke. Many are afraid that if they step out on faith and nothing happens, they will bring reproach to God. That is a yoke. God does not need you to defend His honor. He is God all by Himself. The list of yokes can go on forever. If it prevents you from obeying the voice of the Lord, it is a yoke.

We must allow the anointing God has given us through the infilling of the Holy Ghost to begin to break the yokes in our lives. These yokes are preventing the flow of the Spirit in our lives and not allowing the fountains of the deep to be broken up. If we want the outpouring, we must break open our fountain and let the living water flow through us.

The rain cannot begin until the fountains are broken open. The signs and wonders that flow from each of us through the manifestation of the Holy Ghost in our lives are the critical keys to opening the windows of heaven.

> *Behold, God is great, and we know him not, neither can the number of his years be searched out.*
> *For he maketh small the drops of water: they pour down rain according to the vapour thereof:*
> *Which the clouds do drop and distil upon man abundantly.*
> *Job 36:26-28 (KJV)*

A principle in nature is being explained in this text in Job. The clouds form rain from the drops of water that come from the vapor off the earth. As water evaporates, it floats up and condensates or distills in the clouds. The clouds then accumulate the water into droplets, and gravity allows those droplets to fall to the ground as rain. How amazing.

The same is true in the Spirit. As we begin to allow the living water to flow through us, the outpouring of this water pours into and onto the lives of those around us. As they begin to see our good deeds, they glorify God. As their praise goes up towards heaven,

God responds by pouring out more of His spirit into the vessel that is pouring out His virtue onto the vessels that are giving praise.

The Spiritual rain will fall, according to the amount we break, open the fountains of the deep within ourselves. The greater we open ourselves, the more tremendous the outpouring of the fresh anointing from the presence of God.

So many people are waiting for the outpouring to begin that they fail to see that they are the key to the outpouring. It is time for us to allow the demonstration of the Spirit to flow through us.

We have come a long way from the beginning of this book. Many steps have been taken, and many ideas have been presented. We know that this generation is waiting for the sign of the generation of Noah to manifest. That sign is the church. And more specify the manifestation of the Kingdom of Heaven by the efforts of the church. We know that we can find grace in the eyes of the Lord just as Noah did. We know that God has given us a set of tasks to perform and has promised provision for us to complete those tasks. We know that God has promised to save our sons and daughters. He has made a way for us to become the Sons of God. We know the plan for the manifestation of the Kingdom of Heaven. We know that the rain is coming. We have begun to prepare.

Now the real test is at hand. Are we willing to let the anointing flow through us so we can step out on faith and heal the sick, raise the dead, and open the eyes of the blind and the ears of the deaf? What is our choice going to be?

He has commanded us to teach, preach, heal, cast out devils, forgive, and witness to those we encounter every day. We cannot move into the world until we begin at our Jerusalem. Have we begun to implement this plan?

Today begins the outpouring in your life. God may have to take and break open your life to establish the flow of His presence. Or He may find a more willing servant/son to achieve the goal.

There are current reports from all over the globe of massive healings, people receiving the baptism of the Holy Ghost by the hundreds and thousands. People like Sid Roth, Todd White, David Hoggan, Nik Walker, and many others are testifying of the power of the Holy Ghost, manifesting healing and miracles all over the globe. Revivals and healing in various locations all over the world are happening daily. The Jewel City Revival in Huntington, WV, the Mario Murillo tent revivals in California, and the revival at Asbury University in Wilmore, KY, are just a few examples of the power of God pouring out in our generation. The fountains are starting to break open. The rain is on its way. You can get into the ship and allow the fountain within you to open up, or you can succumb to the flood about to take over this world and be judged as an unfaithful servant.

What is your choice?

Are you ready to be the sign for this Noah generation and be the key to the "revival rain" for your community?

www.ingramcontent.com/pod-product-compliance
Lightning Source LLC
Chambersburg PA
CBHW071244070526
44583CB00017B/2317